The Book of the Mysteries
of the Heavens and the Earth

D1535530

The Book of the Mysteries
of the Heavens and the Earth

and other works of

Bakhayla Mîkâ'êl (Zôsîmâs)

Sir E. A. Wallis Budge
Foreword by R. A. Gilbert

Ibis Press
An imprint of Nicolas-Hays, Inc.
Berwick, Maine

Published in 2004 by
Ibis Press
An imprint of Nicolas-Hays, Inc.
P. O. Box 1126
Berwick, ME 03901-1126
www.nicolashays.com

Distributed to the trade by
Red Wheel/Weiser, LLC
P. O. Box 612
York Beach, ME 03910-0612
www.redwheelweiser.com

Library of Congress Cataloging-in-Publication Data
available on request

Cover design by Phillip Augusta.
Typeset in Caslon
BJ
Printed in the United States of America

10	09	08	07	06	05	04
7	6	5	4	3	2	1

The paper used in this publication meets the minimum requirements of the Ameri-
can National Standard for Information Sciences—Permanence of Paper for Printed
Library Materials Z39.48–1992 (R1997).

CONTENTS

FOREWORD

BEFORE the three "Religions of the Book" began their struggle for the soul of Ethiopia,[1] pagan kings built the city of Axum as their capital. Their gods have gone, but the towering granite obelisks they placed in front of the vanished temples remain. Capped with emblems of the sun and the moon, the obelisks stand as symbolic bridges between earth and sky, silent witnesses to a continuing fascination with the relationship between the heavens and the earth that has been a constant, and powerful, element of Ethiopian spirituality.

Equally powerful has been the legendary history of the kingdom. The Axumite kingdom was actually founded by Sabaean tribes of Semitic origin, who migrated to these African highlands from southern Arabia early in the first millennium B.C. But according to legend, the first king of Ethiopia was Menelik I, the son of Solomon and the Queen of Sheba. Once his kingdom was established, Menelik stole the Ark of the Covenant from Solomon and brought it to Axum, where it remains to this day. Whatever the historical status of the legend—which must be left to personal faith, for there is no objective evidence to support it—it does illustrate neatly the important role played by Judaism in framing the structure and form of Ethiopian Christianity.

The earliest organized religion in Ethiopia was imported from southern Arabia with the Sabaeans during the last centuries before the Christian Era. Their worship centered on a triad of Heaven, Sea, and

---

[1] "Ethiopia" is the name of the country in Amharic, the language of the majority of the people. Because it is the official name, it is used here in preference to the popular, but unofficial, alternative of Abyssinia (which is derived from the Arabic *El Habesha*).

Earth, in the persons of Astar, Beher and Medr, to which they added the tribal god of Aksum, Mahrem, who is identified with Ares (Mars), as Astar is to be identified with the Babylonian Ishtar, associated with the heavens and, in particular, with Venus. The obelisks reflect their worship.

Sabaean religion was not followed immediately by Christianity. Judaism had also entered Ethiopia, partly by way of Jewish traders and others who traveled up the Nile, but principally through the large-scale immigration of Jews from southern Arabia. Jewish communities gained converts from native tribes within the Axumite kingdom, some of whom resisted conversion to Christianity, and whose descendants, the Falashas, still practice a heterodox form of Judaism. This incorporates both pagan and Christian elements and includes acceptance of monasticism: a wholly un-Jewish concept, but a practice common in Christian Ethiopia.

And just as Judaism first reached Ethiopia from Egypt, so did Christianity. Its establishment as the official, and ultimately dominant, religion of the country was due, however, to the activities of Greek Christians early in the fourth century A.D. According to legendary history—supported by patristic texts and more recently discovered inscriptions at Axum—the Axumite king Ezana was converted by Frumentius and Aidesius, the sons of a Greek scholar from Tyre who had traveled to Ethiopia. These two missionaries not only spread the new faith, but also educated Ezana and acted as regents during his youth. This brought official blessings upon Christianity, and about A.D. 330. Frumentius went to Alexandria, where Athanasius, the great champion of Christian orthodoxy, consecrated him as a bishop, gave him the title of "Abuna" (i.e. "Our Father") and confirmed him as Patriarch of the

Ethiopian Church. Frumentius then returned to Ethiopia, and from this time onward the country can be considered effectively a Christian nation. Other troubles, however, lay ahead.

Ethiopia may have been Christian, but what kind of Christian? During the fourth and fifth centuries, the major divisions within Christianity concerned the theological definition of the Person of Christ. To the modern observer, obscure philosophical distinctions in dogmatic theology seem to be of little or no practical concern, but in the early Church they were matters of enormous importance, generating controversies and passions that shook empires as well as souls. The first of these controversies was a violent dispute as to the divinity of Christ. It centered on the teaching of Arius (ca. A.D. 250–ca. 336), who denied that the incarnate Christ was divine. There were major political ramifications to this dispute, in that the western and eastern Roman emperors supported opposing views, but Frumentius—who might have been expected to lean toward the east—followed the lead of Athanasius, who was the great and ultimately successful opponent of Arius, and Ethiopia remained in the orthodox camp. A century later it would leave it.

The second great division came after the Council of Chalcedon, in 451, when a group of eastern churches opposed the definition of the Person of Christ as laid down by the Council. In contrast to the orthodox view, that there are two natures—human and divine—in the Person of the Incarnate Christ, the dissidents argued that in Him there is only one, wholly divine nature. As a consequence of their belief, the dissident churches, which included the Egyptian (Coptic) and Ethiopian churches, were termed Monophysite.[2]

---

[2] From the Greek, μόνος (one) and φύσις (nature).

In the next century, other missionaries—the "nine saints" who probably came from Syria—further strengthened the Christianity of the Axumite empire. Ethiopia was now seen by both halves of the Roman Empire as also being a significant political power on both sides of the Red Sea, a power that could help them contain Persia and control the restless people of Arabia. Accordingly, both Rome and Byzantium sought to bring Ethiopia into their respective religious folds, but the Ethiopian church continued to give allegiance to the Patriarch of Alexandria, who appointed the Ethiopian clergy and determined the main thrust of the church's theology. The ceremonies and observances of the Church, however, were drawn from many sources and formed an amalgam unique to itself.

This might have changed over the centuries, but the rise of Islam in the seventh century and its rapid spread, by way of political conquest, through the Middle East and across North Africa, depleted the Coptic church of Egypt and isolated Ethiopia from the rest of Christendom. Behind the iron curtain of Islam, the Ethiopian church went its own way for more than five hundred years. Despite internal upheavals, Ethiopia resisted Muslim invasion and remained both independent and Christian. In the 13th century, the church experienced both revival and expansion under the great Abuna Takla Hâymanôt, and gradually contact with Western Christianity was renewed. This resulted in Portuguese assistance to repel Muslim invasions in the early 16th century, and a temporary, "official" conversion to Roman Catholicism 100 years later. When this came to an end, the Ethiopian church reverted to Monophysitism and fealty to the Coptic church, but in recent years—since 1959—it has become completely independent. And for more than a thousand years it has also been the inspiration and the mainstay of creativity among its people, who have been responsible for some of the most dramatic art forms and the most remarkable literature to come out of Africa.

The cultural influences on the Ethiopian church, and thus on its literature and art, have been Jewish, Alexandrian, and Syrian. Jewish influences are to be seen in the structure of Ethiopian churches, which are modeled on the Jewish temple: a rectangular holy of holies is surrounded by a circular area in which the believers assemble, while only the serving clergy may enter the central tabernacle on which stands the tabot, a representative copy of the Ark of the Covenant.[3] The church year is also influenced by the Jewish calendar, and both the Sabbath and Sunday are observed as holy days. In addition the use of the Tergum, based on the Jewish Targum, as a method of interpreting the received literature of the orthodox faith in monastic and lay education, is a survival from the pre-Christian Judaic period of the Axumite empire.

Jewish texts also survive in the canon of the Ethiopic Old Testament, which includes such apocryphal works as the Books of Jubilees, Enoch, and Baruch. Interpretation of both these and the truly canonical books uses the Alexandrian allegorical method, and many patristic texts emanating from Alexandria survive in Ethiopian translations from the Greek. Other important Ethiopian texts, notably the Ethiopic *Didascalia*, derive from early Syrian theological works.

But Ethiopian literature was not confined to reworking translations of imported texts. There is an impressive body of original Ethiopian religious texts: legendary histories, lives of saints, and apocalyptic

---

[3] Many churches in Ethiopia are round with thatched roofs. Sometimes, as at Bethlehem near the famous rock churches of Lalibela, a modern thatched structure surrounds and protects an ancient and spectacular tabernacle.

works in particular, with an angelology owing much to Jewish tradition. Many of the surviving copies of these texts—most of which date from the 18th and 19th centuries with only a few from the medieval period—are illustrated in brilliant color with the striking and complex decoration, the ubiquitous crosses, and strange, haunting portraits that are typical of Ethiopian painting.

Nor is Ethiopian literature solely religious. During the enforced isolation of their country from the Western world, the Ethiopian people preserved and developed folk beliefs that owed more to paganism—and sometimes to Islam—than to Christianity. Their Christian faith, however, continued to sit comfortably side-by-side with a belief in demons, protective charms and magical practices, and the art forms to be seen in religious literature flow naturally into magic scrolls and talismans. Such scrolls typically include painted angels, crosses, saints, prophets, kings (especially Solomon), or even Jesus Christ, all bearing specific symbolic significance. However, the accompanying texts are not for worship or devotion: they are prayers or spells to give protection and to ward off evil.

The metaphysical underpinning of these prayers and spells can be found in Ethiopian religious texts: in the lives of the saints, in apocalyptic works such as *The Book of Enoch*, and in compilations such as *The Book of the Mysteries of the Heavens and the Earth*. Sometimes the descriptions of supernatural beings run counter to received opinion and portray them as unusual, as in the account in *The Book of Mysteries* of angels who are clearly male, and have eight wings: two to cover their faces, two to cover their feet, two to cover their hands, and two to cover their penises.

But it is neither their oddity nor their charm that justify the publication of translations of these Ethiopian texts. Part of their value is the light that they shed on early Christian texts, some of which survive only in Ethiopic translation, and one of which, *The Book of Enoch*, gave Ethiopian Christianity one of its distinctive features—a feature more noticeable in folk belief than in orthodox theology. This is an emphasis on sin as originating not only in the disobedience of Adam and Eve, but also in the fallen angels who continue to lead man astray. Ranged against them, also emphasized in *Enoch*, are the archangels, the seraphim and the cherubim who serve as protectors and guardians of humanity, and who are honored with specific festivals in the Ethiopian Church calendar. And who are called upon for assistance in Ethiopian magical practices.

To earlier generations of scholars, texts such as *The Book of the Mysteries of the Heavens and the Earth* were stigmatized as primitive, superstitious, and worthless. Thus the German scholar Hiob Ludolf (1624–1704) was chagrined to find that the text was not the lost *Book of Enoch* and described it—unjustly—as simply a collection of "foolish fables and silly stories." Similarly the Axumite Chronicle, which exists only in texts of the 15th century, was condemned as having no value as an independent historical source. But recent scholarship has demonstrated, by comparing it with patristic sources, that the Chronicle represents much earlier traditions and is of immense value for understanding the early history of Ethiopia. Only by approaching these texts objectively and considering them dispassionately can we benefit from what lies hidden within them.

They are also a significant part of the cultural history of Africa, which has been sadly neglected in the past. And yet, paradoxically, it was the very consigning of African art and literature to the category of "curiosities" that helped to ensure their preservation, just at the time when the traditional societies and cultures in which they arose began their slow but inevitable journey toward extinction.

Ethiopian texts began to arrive in Europe in the late 16th century, and were supplemented two hundred years later by material brought back by James Bruce and other travelers who had gone in search of the sources of the Nile. But it was a by-product of British imperialism that gave scholars access to the full range of Ethiopian literature.

In 1867, in response to the imprisonment and murder of British consular officials by the Emperor Theodore II, a British military expedition invaded Ethiopia. Theodore was defeated (and committed suicide) and the capital, Magdala, was stormed and destroyed in 1868. The British forces then left the country, bearing with them huge quantities of Ethiopian treasures, artifacts, and manuscripts that had been looted from Magdala and elsewhere. These were subsequently dispersed around Britain, although many of them, including the most significant items, found their way into public and private libraries and museums throughout Europe. By the end of the 19th century, the most important of these manuscripts were being carefully edited, annotated, translated, and published.

Within the English-speaking world the most energetic and prolific translator was the keeper (the head) of the Department of Egyptian and Assyrian Antiquities at the British Museum: Ernest Alfred Thompson Wallis Budge. Budge, who was born in 1857, was a natural and gifted linguist. As a student at Oxford he excelled at Semitic languages and published two books on Assyrian texts while still an undergraduate. In 1883, he began his lifelong career at the British Museum as an assistant in the Department of Oriental Antiquities.

Budge was not, however, a desk-bound scholar. Between 1886 and his retirement in 1924 he dug or examined some two dozen archaeological sites in Egypt, the Sudan, and Mesopotamia. He was a keen popularizer of Egyptology, a meticulous editor of texts (helped by an early practical knowledge of printing), and a prolific author with a prodigious output of over 130 original works, editions and translations in his chosen field. Although he is best known as an Egyptologist, Budge was also an authority on Coptic, Syriac, and Ethiopic texts, of which he was a highly-skilled translator.

During his lifetime he published eight translations from Ethiopian texts, beginning with *The Life and Exploits of Alexander the Great* (1896), and ending with a study of *The Alexander Book in Ethiopia* (1933). The most sumptuous were large facsimiles in full color, with translations, of three profusely illustrated texts: *The Lives of Mabâ, Sayôn and Gabra Krestôs* (1898); *The Miracles of the Blessed Virgin Mary*, and the *Life of Hanna* (1900); and *The Life . . . and Miracles of Takla Hâymânôt* (1906).

Budge's extensive work on Syriac and Coptic literature, which have a significant bearing on Ethiopian texts, was carried out largely in what might be called his Middle Period, but toward the end of his life—he died in 1934, eight years after his wife—he concentrated heavily on both the literature and history of Ethiopia. In 1928 he published his *History of Ethiopia (Nubia and Abyssinia)*, closely followed by a major translation of the *Book of the Saints of the Ethiopian Church*. Within a year, he had ventured into more esoteric literature with the publication of *The Bandlet of Righteousness: An Ethiopian Book of the Dead*. Next, he returned to his work on Alexander, and then began his last edition and translation: *The Book of the Mysteries of the Heavens and the Earth*, which he completed but did not live to see in print. It is a fitting text to follow *The Bandlet of Righteousness* and constitutes a fine swan-song for its translator. But it deserves to be recognized as more than a memorial to Budge, for it is a fine expression of Ethiopian spirituality—a facet of human endeavor that is all too likely to be lost as the worst aspects of Western culture over-run its homeland.

R. A. Gilbert
Bristol, England
December 2003

PREFACE

THE present volume contains the complete Ethiopic text and an English translation of a unique Abyssinian vellum manuscript which arrived in EUROPE in the second half of the XVIIth century. Of the sender, and the means by which it was dispatched, no certain knowledge is available. From the life of NICOLAS CLAUDE FABRI, the Seigneur of PEIRESC (1580–1637), by PETER GASSENDI, we know that this manuscript was in the library of Seigneur PEIRESC until his death. PEIRESC was a very learned man; his library was famous in EUROPE, and he was especially interested in ABYSSINIA and its history. By means unknown, the little vellum manuscript passed into the possession of PEIRESC, and as a native title-page stated that it contained the 'Book [of the prophecy of] ENOCH', MAṢḤAFA HÊNÔK መጽሐፈ ፡ ሄኖክ ።, the Seigneur, believing that he owned a literary work of the highest importance, added a second title. When the news spread abroad that the famous lost work of ENOCH had been discovered, it stirred up very considerable interest, and efforts on all sides were made by scholars to learn the contents of the manuscript. Whether PEIRESC could read Ethiopic is unknown, but there seems to be absolutely no doubt that he died in 1637 firmly believing that the little manuscript contained the genuine 'Book of ENOCH', the complete text of which had been lost for centuries.

The interest taken in the PEIRESC manuscript by LUDOLF, the famous Ethiopic scholar, was very great, and having obtained copies of the first and last folios in it, and studied them, he decided that before he could make any answers to his friends as to the contents of the manuscript generally it would be necessary for him to see it in its entirety and to read it through. He went to AQUAE SEXTIAE, PEIRESC'S former seat, only to find that, when the Seigneur died, his great library had been purchased by Cardinal MAZARIN and removed to PARIS. He went to PARIS in 1683, and at length obtained access to the manuscript in the BIBLIOTHECA REGIA. There great disappointment awaited him, for he found that the text in the PEIRESC manuscript was not that of the Book of ENOCH, but that of an unknown work by one BAKHAYLA MÎKÂ'ÊL. The book contained several quotations from the Book of ENOCH, and one section dealt with his birth, but it certainly was not the famous lost 'Book of ENOCH'. LUDOLF allowed his chagrin to overcome his fair-mindedness, and described its contents as a collection of foolish fables and silly stories which were so absurd that he could hardly bear to read them. Apparently he never believed that the 'Book of ENOCH' could exist in ABYSSINIA, and his views about the character of the contents of PEIRESC'S manuscript confirmed his old opinion.

PEIRESC'S manuscript was first accurately described by H. ZOTEN-BERG, the author of the *Catalogue of the Abyssinian MSS. (Gheez and Amharic)* in the BIBLIOTHÈQUE NATIONALE, PARIS, 1877, who numbered it Éth. 37 Peiresc (see *infra*, p. xviii). After the death of PEIRESC the manuscript was neglected, perhaps even ill-treated, and the vellum folios became dirty and dog-eared, and in several places the ink had been rubbed off the vellum; and when it reached ZOTENBERG'S hands there were gaps in the text. ZOTENBERG found that the manuscript contained four distinct compositions, but only the first of these was regarded by the author as a complete book. The title may, however, be held to refer to all four compositions in the manuscript. The first composition is entitled 'The Book of the

Preface

Mysteries of the Heavens and the Earth', and was edited and translated, with the valuable help of GUIDI, by J. PERRUCHON, and printed by GRAFFIN and NAU in *Patrologia Orientalis*, tom. i, fasc. i, PARIS (no date). To include BAKHAYLA MÎKÂ'ÊL'S work in this fine *Corpus* of Oriental theological works was a wise decision, and all Ethiopic scholars will regret that only failing health prevented PERRUCHON from completing his work and publishing all the four compositions in the PEIRESC manuscript.

All the compositions in BAKHAYLA MÎKÂ'ÊL'S work have not the same value, but each of them is of great importance, and every student who has studied the first of them must have regretted that they were not printed together with it in one volume. Having perused carefully PERRUCHON'S text, I decided to obtain, if possible, copies of the text of the other sections of PEIRESC'S manuscript in order to find out how they were connected with it, or if they had any connexions at all. I applied to the Director of the BIBLIOTHÈQUE NATIONALE in PARIS asking his permission to have a rotographic copy made, and with great promptness and courtesy he sent on my application to the proper quarter, and in a week or ten days the rotograph arrived. It was clear that PERRUCHON or GUIDI had found means to fill the lacunae, and to complete broken words and to correct misreadings. ZOTENBERG told us (see his *Catalogue*, p. 140) that J. M. VANSLEB made a complete copy of the PEIRESC manuscript in 1670, which is now preserved with its original in the BIBLIOTHÈQUE NATIONALE, and the notes in PERRUCHON'S printed text showed that he had made use of VANSLEB'S copy. A collation of the printed text of PERRUCHON with that of the rotograph proved that VANSLEB did not always reproduce the spellings of the original, and that in some places he did not know the exact meaning of the text before him. And in some passages he paraphrases parts of sentences, and adds glosses of words which were either foreign or unknown to him.

It seemed to me that many other students would like to have the second, third, and fourth compositions in the PEIRESC manuscript available in a handy form, and therefore I decided to reproduce all the original texts with English translations. The authorities of the BIBLIOTHÈQUE NATIONALE most kindly acceded to my request for a rotograph copy of the VANSLEB transcript of the PEIRESC manuscript. When this came to hand I consulted DR. JOHN JOHNSON, Printer to the University of OXFORD, about the reproduction of a complete facsimile text.

The rotograph of the PEIRESC manuscript showed that its writer, or copyist, was not a professional scribe, and that he had made many mistakes in copying, and that many words lacked syllables and letters. Omitted words and letters were written in minuscules above the words to which they belonged, and with inks of different colours, and in some cases they are illegible. Figures and the name of the VIRGIN were written in red, but in the photographs they appeared as black smudges. With the help of the rotograph of the VANSLEB transcript, and the expert knowledge and methods of the OXFORD artists and photographers, it became possible to fill up many of the gaps in the Ethiopic texts, and decipher the illegible lines at the corners of the folios. Many collations of the rotographs with the photographic bases of the plates were made, and I believe that the Ethiopic texts printed in this book are as nearly correct as we are ever likely to have them, or until a better-written and more accurate manuscript is found. I believe that all students of the PEIRESC manuscript will welcome the publication of copies of the texts as complete and accurate as photography can make them, and

Preface

free from the mistakes and misreadings, both of editors and compositors, which are always found in transcripts printed from types. We owe these copies to the special interest and care which has been devoted to their production by DR. JOHN JOHNSON, Printer to the University of OXFORD, and to the skill and experience of MR. E. ELDRIDGE and the other members of his staff. To the readers of the English portion of this book I am indebted for many helpful suggestions.

E. A. WALLIS BUDGE

48 BLOOMSBURY STREET,
BEDFORD SQUARE,
LONDON, W.C. I.
November 1934.

PUBLISHER'S NOTE

Sir E. A. Wallis Budge died on 23 November 1934, and was therefore unable to see this book through the final stages of its production

INTRODUCTION

EARLY in the second half of the XVIIth century the third edition of the life of NICOLAS CLAUDE FABRI, the famous Seigneur of PEIRESC (born 1580, died 1637), written by PETER GASSENDI (born Jan. 21, 1502; died Oct. 10, 1592) of CHARTERSIER in PROVENCE, Professor of Mathematics and Philosophy in FRANCE, was published.[1] Now PEIRESC was in close communication with friends and officials in ABYSSINIA, and he was well acquainted with the phenomenal success of VERMELLIUS, a jeweller who had turned soldier, and who at the head of 8,000 troops only had won a great battle for the King of ABYSSINIA. The King's army, 50,000 strong, was unable to do what VERMELLIUS had done with his 8,000 men, who were equipped with European weapons. The Abyssinian Court had been delighted with his jewellery and his striking victory, and the King made him Commander-in-Chief of his army. VERMELLIUS then wrote to his friends in MARSEILLES and begged them to send him European books to help him in developing his plans. What answer they made is not known, but PEIRESC knew that they would not do much to help VERMELLIUS, and he therefore at his own expense dispatched to ABYSSINIA a large number of books including, with special care, mathematical works, and books dealing with military and civil architecture with numerous plans and diagrams. It follows, as Professor GASSENDI says, that PEIRESC, feeling that his gifts would be received gratefully, felt himself free to ask VERMELLIUS to send him in return a number of Abyssinian or Ethiopic books, and written descriptions of the country, and of the rites and religion and manners and customs of the country and people, about all of

[1] *Viri illustris Nicolai Claudii Fabricii de Peiresc Senatoris Aquisextensis vita*, Hagae comitum, 1655.

which little definite information existed in EUROPE.[1] This is very prob-
able in the light of further information, but we have no proof of it.

At another place in the life of PEIRESC by Professor GASSENDI, we
are told that a certain Capuchin called GILLES DE LOCHES,[2] who had
on many occasions received assistance from PEIRESC, went to AIX to
visit his patron in 1633. GILLES had been travelling in EGYPT for
seven years, and had visited many of the monasteries there and
examined their libraries. In the course of his description of the
manuscripts which he had seen he said that he had found a manuscript which was entitled MAZHAFAHAT EINOK, that is to say the Book
[of the Prophecy] of ENOCH,[3] which contained an account of everything which would happen up to the end of the world. He declared
that this book was written in the Abyssinian or Ethiopic script and
language, and that the Book of ENOCH, although absolutely unknown
in EUROPE, was preserved in its integrity among the ABYSSINIANS.[4]

PEIRESC was so carried away by the eloquence of GILLES the
Capuchin, that he forthwith determined to obtain a copy of the
Book of ENOCH, no matter what amount of labour its acquisition
cost him, or what amount of money he was obliged to spend in
satisfying his desire.[5]

We have seen that PEIRESC, when he sent out books, &c., to VER-
MELLIUS of MONTPELLIER, the Commander-in-Chief of the Army of

[1] 'Cum confidisset autem illum gratissime id accepturum, licere opinatus est petere
ab eo libros aliquot Æthiopicos, inscriptiones obvias, descriptionem Amarae montis,
itemque rituum, religionis, vasorum et similium quae Europaeis sciret ignota'
(Gassendi, *Vita*, p. 171).

[2] Ludolf has 'Ægidio Lochiensi' (*Historia*, p. 347).

[3] More correctly Maṣḥafa Hênôk መጽሐፈ፡ ሄኖክ፡

[4] 'Quandoquidem vero inter caetera animadvertisse se dixit *Mazhafahat Einok*
seu *Prophetiam Enochi* declarantem ea quae ad finem usque saeculi eventura sunt,
librum Europae pridem invisum, illeic euntem charactere et idiomate Æthiopico, seu
Abyssinorum, apud quos is fuerat servatus' (p. 168).

[5] His biographer says: 'Ideo Pereskius sic fuit accensus eius, quoquo pretio com-
parandi studio, et nullis parcens sumptibus, ipsum denique sui faceret juris' (p. 169).

the King of ABYSSINIA, asked for books, &c., to be sent back to him in return. Whether he specially mentioned the names of any Ethiopian works is not known. But, having learned from the Capuchin that the Book of ENOCH existed in ABYSSINIA, it is tolerably certain that he wrote to his friend VERMELLIUS and asked him to procure him a copy. Be this as it may, we know that between 1633 and 1637 PEIRESC received from ABYSSINIA an Ethiopic manuscript sent presumably to him by VERMELLIUS or by some official at his instigation. PEIRESC received the manuscript with great pleasure, and had it rebound and placed it in his large and splendid library, and regarded it as a priceless treasure. When the manuscript arrived it was bound in the usual Abyssinian fashion between two wooden boards and, according to its wrapper or some kind of covering, it purported to contain the Book of the Prophecy of ENOCH. PEIRESC added a second covering elaborately ornamented with gold and the label 'Revelationes Henochi Aethiopice'. PEIRESC rejoiced in his acquisition, though there is no evidence that he could read Ethiopic, and he died in 1637 firmly believing that the book which he had obtained with such difficulty was the famous Book of ENOCH, the supposed loss of which had been lamented by theologians for many centuries.

The fame of PEIRESC's Ethiopic manuscript spread rapidly among the learned, and LUDOLF, the great Ethiopic scholar, was urged by his friends to give them some account of it. This he was very anxious to do, for the mention of the Book of ENOCH in the life of PEIRESC interested him greatly. In his *History of Ethiopia* (p. 347) he says that he spared neither toil nor expense until he obtained copies of passages from the beginning, middle, and end of PEIRESC's manuscript. He first made a journey from FRANKFORT to AIX in PROVENCE, which he calls Aquae Sextiae, where PEIRESC had lived formerly, but he found that he was dead and that his magnificent library had been purchased by Cardinal MAZARIN and removed to PARIS. In 1683 LUDOLF went to PARIS to consult the manuscript in the Cardinal's library, and found that it had been transferred to the BIBLIOTHECA REGIA; there he went and it was placed in his hands. On examining the text he found that the manuscript did *not* contain the Book of ENOCH, as the gilded title stated, but a work which had been written by one BAKHAYLA MÎKÂ'ÊL በኂደስ፡ ሚካኤል፡ Many of the passages in it were identical with the extracts which JOSEPH SCALIGER had found in the book of GEORGE the SYNCELLUS,[1] which was also called the Book of ENOCH. The writer of the latter frequently quoted ENOCH, and one section dealt with the birth of ENOCH; from this section the book had probably obtained its name among careless or ignorant scribes. The sender of the manuscript to PEIRESC was himself probably deceived and, thinking that it contained the real Book of ENOCH, sent it to FRANCE.

The disappointment of LUDOLF and theologians in general on the discovery that PEIRESC'S manuscript did not contain the Book of ENOCH was very great, for it was believed that the work would throw much light on problems connected with the criticism of the New Testament. The Book of ENOCH was well known to all the writers of the New Testament, and many of them were, as their writings testify, influenced by its thought and diction.[2] It is quoted as a genuine production by St. JUDE and as Scripture by St. BARNABAS, and it is frequently quoted as a canonical book by many of the Fathers and Apologists of the IInd and IIIrd centuries of our Era. A couple of centuries later, possibly because copies of it became scarce, its prophetic value became discredited, and soon after it fell under the ban of the Church. The long passages from it quoted in

---

[1] i.e. his *Chronography* which was written about A.D. 800.
[2] See an interesting section of the General Introduction to the translation of the Book of Enoch by the Rev. R. H. Charles (Oxford, 1893), p. 41 f.

Greek by GEORGE the SYNCELLUS suggest that he was aware that all his readers were not in possession of copies of the Book. During the Middle Ages the Book of ENOCH, so far as the original text was concerned, whether Hebrew or Greek, was believed to be lost. In the third quarter of the XVIIIth century the news reached ENGLAND that BRUCE, the great Oriental traveller, had discovered an Ethiopic version of the book in ABYSSINIA; he acquired two ancient manuscripts of the work, and had a copy of one of them made by a careful scribe. The text has been edited and translated by R. LAWRENCE, *Book of Enoch*, OXFORD, 1821; HOFFMANN, *Das Buch Henoch*, JENA, 1833; DILLMANN, *Liber Henoch*, LEIPZIG, 1851 and 1853; CHARLES, *Book of Enoch*, OXFORD, 1893.

LUDOLF read through the manuscript which had been sent to PEIRESC from cover to cover, but entirely misunderstood its character. He thought that the valuable collections of legends contained in it, which BAKHAYLA MÎKÂ'ÊL had collected from very ancient sources in Greek, or Hebrew, or both, were so stupid and silly that he could hardly find patience to read them.[1] In his *History of Ethiopia* he printed three extracts from the PEIRESC manuscript, and having condemned its contents as 'futiles et absurdissimae narrationes', took no further trouble about the book, except to regard it with a kind of contempt. And he makes it quite clear in his *Historia* that he did not believe in the existence of the Book of ENOCH in ETHIOPIA.

The manuscript sent to PEIRESC passed into the library of Cardinal MAZARIN and finally into the Royal Library, and it now forms No. 117[2] of the BIBLIOTHÈQUE NATIONALE in PARIS. The first full description of it and its contents was published by H. ZOTENBERG, *Catalogue des Manuscrits Éthiopiens (Gheez et Amharique) de la*

---

[1] 'Verum tam crassas et putidas fabulas continet, ut vix legere sustinuerim ' (p. 347).
[2] Also Éth. 37 Peiresc.

Vansleb's Copy of the Peiresc Manuscript

Bibliothèque Nationale, PARIS, 1877, pp. 137 ff. It consisted of 83 vellum leaves[1] measuring 165 × 140 cm. Each page contains two columns of Ethiopic text, but the number of lines to the column varies from 17 (fols. 2–8) to 23 (fols. 73–80). Several columns (e.g. fols. 12, 13) have only 22 lines to the column. Fol. 1*a* has a decorative head-piece with a design characteristically Ethiopian. ZOTENBERG assigned the manuscript to the XVIth century, but I believe that it was written in the first half of the XVth century, and the form of the letter ሎ supports this view. The text of this manuscript contains many mistakes. Single letters, parts of words, whole words, and portions of sentences are sometimes omitted; some of these have been inserted in very small characters between the lines either by the original scribe or some learned reader, but they are often illegible. Many of the numbers are written in red or yellow ink, and are also illegible.

As the result of disappointment, irritation, and haste, LUDOLF called the contents of PEIRESC'S manuscript 'sweepings' or 'rubbish' (*quisquiliae*), but fortunately his wrong and unjust opinion was not shared by all the learned men of his day. The famous Orientalist, JOHN MICHAEL VANSLEB thought the book of such interest and importance that in the year 1670 he made a complete copy of the text with his own hand. This copy is preserved in the BIBLIOTHÈQUE NATIONALE in PARIS where it bears the number 118 (Éth. 36.— Colbert 4407).[2] The little volume measures 205 × 157 mm., and contains 143 folios; each page is filled with a single column of text containing from 24 to 26 lines. At some period after the death of PEIRESC his manuscript suffered rough treatment, and the folios became dirty and dog-eared, and in several places the ink was rubbed off the vellum, and gaps appeared in the text. As the manu-

---

[1] Originally 85 leaves, but fols. 84 and 85 only contained Ethiopic notes which formed no part of the manuscript.   [2] See Zotenberg, *Catalogue*, p. 140.

Bakhayla Mîkâ'êl's Book of Mysteries

script is unique, but for the existence of VANSLEB's copy these lacunae could never have been filled up. With the help of this PERRUCHON and myself have been enabled to reproduce the text in an almost complete state, and also to read many portions of it which were practically illegible. In some cases VANSLEB supplied in his copy words which the scribe of PEIRESC's text had omitted. There are, of course, mistakes in VANSLEB's copy, but these are easily corrected by the readings of PEIRESC's manuscript. VANSLEB's copy has been extremely useful in supplying the illegible or obliterated words on the dog-eared pages of PEIRESC's manuscript, and all those who study the text of that little unique volume will rejoice that the copy was made.

[BAKHAYLA MÎKÂ'ÊL AND HIS WORK]

Of BAKHAYLA MÎKÂ'ÊL, possibly also known as BAṢALÔTA MÎKÂ'ÊL [1] and ZÔSÎMÂS, nothing is known. In a general manner his work suggests that it was the product of the XVth century, although parts of it may be older. M. NAU is undoubtedly correct in refusing to identify him with the famous monk of the same name who flourished in the XIIIth century, and who was believed to have received many remarkable revelations. The manuscript of PEIRESC contains four distinct works, but only the first of them is treated by the author as a complete book. And it is therefore uncertain whether the title of the book given at the beginning of the text is intended to refer to Part I or to all four Parts. Part I. This title reads, MAṢḤAFA MEŠṬÎRA SAMÂY WAMEDER, መጽሐፈ፡ ምሥጢረ፡ ሰማይ፡ ወምድር፡ 'The Book of the Mysteries of the Heavens and the Earth' (Fol. 1a). The author continues, 'which describeth the First Tabernacle and the later one, and maketh known the mystery of all creation, and how every created thing was created in its kind.

---

[1] See Perruchon, *Le Livre des Mystères*, Paris (no date), p. x, note 7.

The Contents of Bakhayla Mîkâ'êl's Work

Abbâ BAKHAYLA MÎKÂ'ÊL taught this, and he was made to understand [the mysteries] by the marvellous beings[1] (?) of the heavens.' In other words, BAKHAYLA MÎKÂ'ÊL states that the information he gives was derived from celestial beings. This Part begins on Fol. 1*a* and ends on Fol. 48*b*, col. 2, l. 14, where it is said: 'Is ended the description of the mysteries'. The complete text of Part I was published together with a French translation by the eminent Ethiopist J. PERRUCHON in *Patrologia Orientalis* (ed. GRAFFIN and NAU), tom. i, fasc. 1, PARIS (no date). Owing to the failure of his eyesight M. PERRUCHON was unable to complete the work, but with the help of Professor D. IGNAZIO GUIDI the proofs were passed for press and happily the book appeared. PERRUCHON thought that Part I was a work complete in itself, and apparently he made no attempt to edit and translate Parts II–IV.

Part II. TERGÂMÊ RÛ'ĚYÛ LA-YÔḤANES ትርጓሜ ፡ ራእዩ ፡ በየሐንስ ፡ 'Interpretation of the Vision of JOHN', i.e. the Book of the Apocalypse (Fol. 48*b*, col. 1). The colophon states that this section is to be recited during Passion Week, during the festival of Mount TABOR, and during the festival of St. MICHAEL. Copies of it were only to be found in the city of [name erased] and in DENKUENÂ ደንኩና ፡

Part III. NAGAR BA'ĚNTA MESṬÎRA MALAKÔT ነገር ፡ በእንተ ፡ ምስጢረ ፡ መለኮት ። 'Discourse concerning the Mystery of the Godhead' (Fol. 70*b*, col. 2). The last section of this Part was written by ISAAC, the son of BAṢALÔTA MÎKÂ'ÊL.

Part IV. KAL'A NAGARA BA'ĚNTA LEDATÛ LA-HÊNÔK ካልእ ፡ ነገር ፡ በእንተ ፡ ልደቱ ፡ ለሄኖክ ። 'Another Discourse concerning the Birth of ENOCH' (Fol. 76*b*, col. 2).

On fol. 83*a* is the following note: 'Perlegit et examinavit hunc librum erroresque notabiliores correxit Fr. JOH. MICHAEL VANSLEBIUS. Ord. Praed. 1670.

---

[1] See Perruchon, op. cit., p. 1, note 2.

PART I

Summary of Contents

Day 4. Creation of the sun, moon, and stars. The light of the sun was reduced one half.

The rebellion of SEṬNÂ'ÊL.

The battle in heaven: SEṬNÂ'ÊL makes war on God.

Defeat and final victory of the angels of God.

Description of SEṬNÂ'ÊL.

„ 5. Creation of BĔHÊMÔT, LÊWYÂTÂN, and birds and fishes.

The birds which produce pearls.

„ 6. Creation of the beasts of the desert and field.

Creation of ADAM whom God mounted on an elephant.

MICHAEL and the Seraphim welcome ADAM.

MICHAEL brings a man out of hell.

How SATAN entered Paradise on the back of a camel.

The forbidden Tree.

The Tree of Life and CHRIST.

The angels which became men and sinned.

The works and occupations of the angels.

The Flood caused by the wickedness of men.

The destruction of the giants and the Flood.

The building of the Tower of BABEL.

The languages and nations of the children of SHEM.

The languages and nations of the children of HAM.

The languages and nations of the children of JAPHET.

The history of ABRAHAM.

ABRAHAM talks with God.

Circumcision of ABRAHAM.

God's speech to ABRAHAM.

St. MICHAEL led the MAGI to PALESTINE, and brought the ISRAELITES through the RED SEA.

PHARAOH and his horse.

Wonders wrought by God.

The number Seven.

The Genealogy of the Fathers.

JOSEPH flies to a tree for protection.

2

Summary of Contents

Summary of Contents

The Law renewed.
The Eighth Area.
The Ninth Area.
The Tree REMÂN.
The Tenth Area.
The Eleventh Area.
The Twelfth Area.
The Thirteenth Area.
The Fourteenth Area.
The Fifteenth Area.
The Sixteenth Area with explanation by MOSES and AARON.
The effigies of the saints and patriarchs.
The Seventeenth Area, with an explanation.
The settlements of the Twelve Tribes.
The stones symbolic of the Twelve Tribes.
The meanings of these stones.
The three pillars and their names.
The Sign of the Cross.
The Law and Books of MOSES.
The Four Cherubim.
The beloved vine of ISRAEL.
The Festivals of ISRAEL, with an explanation.
The Resurrection, with an explanation.
The eagle at LEBANON.
The Incarnation, with an explanation.
The trees of Paradise.
The tree on which CHRIST was crucified.
The forms of CHRIST after the Resurrection.
The Abode of Souls.
The Angel of Death.
The Vision of CHRIST seen by the saints.
The beasts seen by DANIEL.
DANIEL and ALEXANDER THE GREAT.
The eagle seen by EZRA.

4

Summary of Contents

Concerning ANTICHRIST.

The Day of Judgement.

The Apostles and the division of the world.

Our Lord addresses the Disciples.

The decision of the Apostles after the Ascension.

The temptations of St. ANTHONY.

The Coming of our Lord and ANTICHRIST.

IN THE NAME OF THE FATHER, AND THE SON, AND THE HOLY GHOST,
ONE GOD!

[THE TITLE OF THE BOOK, SUMMARY OF ITS CONTENTS, AND THE
NAME OF ITS AUTHOR]

[Fol. 1a, col. 1.] And this is the BOOK OF THE MYSTERY OF THE HEAVENS AND THE EARTH which relateth the mystery (*or*, mysteries) of the First Tabernacle and the Last [Tabernacle], which maketh known the mystery of all created things, how they were created each according to its species [*or*, one following the other]. Thus taught 'Abbâ BAKHAYLA MÎKÂ'ÊL and he had understanding [Fol. 1a, col. 2] from the admirable beings of the heavens (?).[1]

And the angel who had been sent unto him was GABRIEL, the shining one of light, and he said unto him, 'Hearken. I will relate unto thee everything from the beginning and I will make thee to know how each and every thing followed in succession.'

[1] Ludolf translated *tamhâna samây* ተማህነ ፡ ሰማይ as a proper name (*Historiam Aethiopicam*, p. 347, No. XXXIV, at the foot). Perruchon followed him, but saw that this rendering was doubtful because the root *tâmâh* does not exist in Ethiopic, and so was prepared to offer as an alternative for the proper name 'les merveilles du ciel.' But as we are told that the archangel Gabriel, 'the brilliant shining one', spoke to the author, it seems to me better to read 'admirable ones' instead of 'marvels of the heavens.' In speaking of the fourth section of the Paris MS., which deals with the birth of Enoch, Ludolf says that it contains stupid and silly fables which he can hardly bear to read—'tam crassas et putidas fabulas continet, ut vix legere sustinuerim'—but it is not clear whether he refers to the fourth section or to all four sections of the manuscript.

The Speech of Gabriel

The Father did not exist before the Son, and the Son did not exist before the Father, and the Holy Ghost did not exist before the Father and [Fol. 1b, col. 1] the Son.

Their state of being preceded the creation of the world, and their state of being was one (i.e. the same) after the creation of the world.[1]

The Names of the Three of them meaneth 'EGZÎ'BEḤÊR (i.e. God), equal in their divinity, and their state of being was one before the heavens and the earth.

There was never a time when they did not exist and their state of being never had a beginning, and their state of being shall never have an end.

They make every one to understand but there is no one who [Fol. 1b, col. 2] can make [any one] to understand them. They have knowledge of everything, but there is no man who knoweth them. They see every one but no man seeth them. They have firm hold of every one but no one hath any hold upon them.

How is it possible for me to tell the story of the greatness of the generousness (or, goodness) of the Creator?

How is it possible for me [to describe] the Creation which He hath created? For it is impossible for that which He doeth to be described adequately and the extent of His capability to be declared.

Praise be unto Thee, O Sea of mercy and humility!

On the man whom He chooseth [Fol. 2a, col. 1] He sheweth mercy; and on the man He chooseth He inflicteth punishment.

[Praise be unto Thee], O Sea of grace and majesty!

To him whom He chooseth He giveth grace and majesty, and well-pleasingness.

---

[1] By making the sentence begin with አሕዱ ፡ ውእቱ ፡ it is possible to read, 'their being was one before the creation of the world and one after the creation of the world'.

The Future of the World was decided at the Creation

[Praise be unto Thee], O Sea of wisdom and knowledge!
To him whom He choseth He giveth wisdom and knowledge.
[Praise be unto Thee], O Sea of gentleness and compassion!
To him whom He choseth, He giveth purity of heart.
[Praise be unto Thee], O Sea of glory and riches!

To him whom He choseth He endoweth with riches, and with honour; [to him whom He choseth] He maketh an uncovering (i.e. maketh revelations).

Since the Scriptures say unto thee [Fol. 2a, col. 2] 'before the world', that is to say, before ADAM, there was no world before ADAM. 'And when ADAM was created' the 'ÔRÎT (i.e. the TÔRÂH or the Pentateuch) saith unto thee, 'the heavens and the earth were finished'; and God finished all the world, having worked out His work. And about this statement the Scriptures agree.

The inheritance of the righteous and the doom of those who deny God (or, the infidels) were created on the first day, even as the [Pentateuch] saith, 'When He made the heavens and the earth' He decided beforehand the future of the world, [Fol. 2b, col. 1] that is to say, for ADAM's judgement and his punishment. Now, the Garden (i.e. Paradise) was created on the third day (Tuesday), and from this [it is clear] that the inheritance of the righteous was created on the first day of the week (Sunday).

And observe well that the kingdom of the heavens was created on the first day of the week; now the kingdom of the heavens means the JERUSALEM of the Heavens which at a later time shall be opened out for the righteous. And PETER said unto our Lord, 'There is nothing which was created [Fol. 2b, col. 2] before the heavens and the earth' (Matthew xxv. 34). And when the Gospel saith unto thee, 'Come ye, ye blessed ones of My Father, inherit the kingdom which was prepared before the world was created', thou must not imagine [that the kingdom was prepared] before the heavens and the earth.

7

The Existence of the Trinity assumed throughout the Pentateuch

For nothing at all existed before the heavens and the earth with the exception of the Three Names, which are 'Father,' 'Son,' and 'Holy Ghost.'

[THE FIRST DAY OF CREATION]

And on the first day our God ('AMLÂK) created the heaven which is called GÊRGÊL. And that [this] heaven is His throne [Fol. 3*a*, col. 1] hearken unto that which ÎSÂYYÂS (ISAIAH) saith: 'The heaven is His throne, and the earth is the resting place of His feet' (Isaiah lxvi. 1). This heaven He made out of white *barad* (literally *ice*, but crystal is meant), even as EZEKIEL saith, 'I saw heaven, which was like unto ice, spread out over the head[s] of the animals' (Ezekiel i. 22). And as for the ice, whence did He create it? He alone knoweth His own hidden matters (*or*, secrets). Let all of us say, 'There is nothing which is too difficult for 'EGZÎ'BEḤÊR.' And thou must not imagine that he began to create [Fol. 3*a*, col. 2] first at the lower part of it, but at the upper.

Now MOSES saith in the beginning of the Pentateuch, 'In the beginning God made the heavens, and the earth existed of old, and the Spirit of God hovered over the water' (Genesis i. 1, 2).

Now, observe well that the Trinity maketh itself apparent in the beginning of the Pentateuch. In respect of the Son the Scriptures call Him the 'First One '; and they say 'God' meaning the Father [Fol. 3*b*, col. 1]; and they say 'Earth' meaning ADAM, who was in the mind (*or*, thought) of God aforetime; and as for the Holy Ghost, the Pentateuch speaketh clearly, saying, 'The Spirit of God moved (*or*, hovered) above the waters.' And the whole of the work of the Pentateuch, and the whole of the narrative of the Pentateuch is [founded] on the Trinity. And the Pentateuch speaketh this statement: 'We will make man in our likeness' (Genesis i. 26). Now observe that the Pentateuch indicateth the Trinity by this passage. And it also saith, 'Come ye, we will see what the children of men

8

[Fol. 3*b*, col. 2] have done' (Genesis xi. 7). Now observe that by this passage the Pentateuch indicateth the Trinity. Observe then that the Pentateuch indicateth [the existence] of the Trinity from the very beginning.

[THE SECOND DAY OF CREATION]

Now let us return to the narrative of the Creation.

On the second day God created the [second] heaven out of fog (*or*, mist) and He called it 'ÊRÂR. Whence did He create the fog? He alone knoweth His own secrets (*or*, hidden things).

[THE THIRD DAY OF CREATION]

And the third heaven was created out of fire, and God called it RÊMÂ and sanctified it.

[THE FOURTH DAY OF CREATION]

Now the fourth heaven He made [also] out of fire. And the colour thereof is [Fol. 4*a*, col. 1] like that of the gem of the sea (i.e. the pearl). He built it of *karkĕdên* (chalcedony) and with twelve precious gems (*or*, pearls?), and one of the gates thereof is one thousand times wider than this world. And if [only] one of the gates thereof is wider than this world, how spacious must the whole of this heaven be! And he who was sent [unto me] said unto me, 'God only knoweth the extent thereof.' And twelve angels keep guard over it. And the gate of the gates[1] hath variegated colour. And the openings in the wall (i.e. windows) [Fol. 4*a*, col. 2] are like sunlight. The vault thereof is lofty, and the roof thereof is painted a deep red colour. And the four sides(?) of it are like unto the *ferem* tree which hath the colour of the heavens, and the . . . thereof are like unto the moon when it is at its full. Inside it is a representation[2] of the creation [as large as] seven suns, or twelve, or four, or the stars.

---

[1] The main gate?

[2] *Or*, model, *or*, picture.

The Treasure-house and Arsenal of the Fourth Heaven

And here is the image of the Shining Face. Before God had created [Fol. 4*b*, col. 1] ADAM the chosen ones (i.e. the beatified) were depicted there, according to what Wisdom saith, 'The righteousness of those who are there depicted shall never be forgotten in respect of them.' And here is the Altar of fire, and here is the TÂBÔT (Ark) of fire, and here are the Seven Tabernacles of fire, and here are the Seven Seas of light, and here are the Vestments of light, and here are the Crowns of light, and here are the Garlands (*or*, tiaras) of Beauty, and here are the Firmly-established Thrones, and here are the Horses [both] white [Fol. 4*b*, col. 2] and red, and here are the Spears of light, and here are the Swords of light, and here are Coats of mail of light, and here are the Shields of light. And here are the Javelins and Daggers of fire, and here are the Arrows and Darts of fire. And here is the Cross of light, and the Censers of light, and the Trees of light. And all these things are in the Fourth Heaven, which is JERUSALEM [Fol. 5*a*, col. 1]. And again He did not show them to the angels after His birth in the flesh and He did not bring them to man before He had put on flesh.

Glory be to Him who hath revealed what we have heard of His wonders, and to the Spirit Who sanctifieth everything.

[THE FIFTH DAY OF CREATION]

And He created the Fifth Heaven out of water, and called it 'LÊWÊN'.

[THE SIXTH DAY OF CREATION]

And He created the Sixth Heaven out of water and called it 'DÎRÎ ̱KÔN'. This heaven which the eyes of men look at is made out of water [Fol. 5*a*, col. 2]. Three heavens have been created out of water, even as our Lord said unto PETER, saying, 'We took pure water and we have created three heavens.' But the Scriptures say unto us, 'In the beginning God created the heavens, and the earth,

Water already in existence when God created the Heavens
and the fire, and the wind, and the light, and the companies of the
holy angels.' These were the creatures which God created on the
first day of the week.

Now, inasmuch as He saith, 'We took the water and we created the
heavens' [Fol. 5*b*, col. 1], was the water created by Him before He
created the heavens? The Scriptures do not say that the water was
created before the heavens, [therefore] what can we say [about the
matter]? He alone knoweth His own hidden things.

And the angels were created from a flame of fire, and each [rank]
of them hath its own language. And as the languages of the children
of ADAM are many, and their countries [are different], so the angels
have many languages, even as the countries of the children of men
are many. And an angel is able to make his fellow angel understand
[Fol. 5*b*, col. 2] him, and [if] he saith unto him, 'Whence comest
thou?' [his fellow angel answereth,] 'From so and so.'

And as the languages of the [groups of] angels are different, in
the same manner their praises are different. Three [ranks] say
'Holy', and three say, 'Glorious (*or*, Praised) [art Thou]', and three
say, 'Thanks be [to Thee]', and three say what the ear of mortal man
cannot bear the hearing of.

[THE ANGELS OF THE FIRST HOUR]

And thou must not imagine that [all] the angels were created at
one time. The Angels of the Face, who belong to the kin of MICHAEL,
were created at the first hour of the day, and as MICHAEL, the Archangel, is faithful (*or*, trustworthy), they press forward to be the first
in [Fol. 6*a*, col. 1] coming to help us.

[THE ANGELS OF THE SECOND HOUR]

And in the second hour the Angels of the Liturgy, that is to say
the Priests, were created.

Creation of the Ten Orders of Angels

[THE ANGELS OF THE THIRD HOUR]

And in the third hour the Thrones were created.

[THE ANGELS OF THE FOURTH HOUR]

And in the fourth hour the SELṬÂNÂT (Dominions) were created.

[THE ANGELS OF THE FIFTH HOUR]

And in the fifth hour the 'AGÂ'ĔZET (Lords) were created.

[THE ANGELS OF THE SIXTH HOUR]

And in the sixth hour the KHAYLÂT (Powers) were created.

[THE ANGELS OF THE SEVENTH HOUR]

And in the seventh hour the RABAWÂT (Tens of thousands) were created.

[THE ANGELS OF THE EIGHTH HOUR]

And in the eighth hour the MAKWÂNENET (Governors or Magistrates) were created.

[THE ANGELS OF THE NINTH HOUR]

And in the ninth hour the 'ARBÂB (Masters?) were created.

[THE SATANIC ANGELS]

And before all the angels which fill the tenth Rank He created the tribe (*or*, kin) of SEṬNÂ'ÊL.

[THE EXCELLENCE OF GOD'S WORKS]

Every work of our God ('AMLÂK) hath been made with wisdom and craftsmanship. And we all having heard this, say, 'Thou art able to perform everything, and there is nothing which is too difficult [Fol. 6*a*, col. 2] for Thee to do.' His work is a marvel of the skill

Sî'ôl (Shî'ôl) under the Rocky Bed of the World-Ocean

of the handicraftsman. That which hath not yet been written (i.e. described) is more marvellous than that which hath been narrated. But the contents of the Eighty-one Books have told us as much as we are able to hear, and our soul gaineth strength from all created things, and it is bound to the word of God.

[THE STORY OF THE CREATION—*continued*]

Let us return to the creation of the earth. Like the Seven Heavens the earth also hath been made out of water, even as the apostle PETER saith, 'As for the earth God created it out of water, and stablished it firmly by the word of God' [Fol. 6*b*, col. 1]. Beneath it He created a great female sea, a subdivision of the male water which is in the heavens. This earth is above the water, and, below the Ocean (WEḲYÂNÔS), is the awful abyss of water, and below the abyss is a rock, and below the rock is Sî'ôL (SHEOL), and below sî'ôL is the wind, and under the wind is the boundary of darkness.

And beyond this [boundary] what is there? God alone knoweth His hidden things. But the Holy Spirit hath consecrated(?) these things [therefore] let us leave [the consideration of] this question to some one else [Fol. 7*b*, col. 2]. God hath consecrated(?) sî'ôL according to its natural character, since the Spirit hath not sanctified everything; moreover, the earth itself hath not the power to carry all created things.

Now as concerneth the length (height?) of the heavens, it is six times higher(?) than our heaven, and it is twice as high(?) as that of the earth which we see. And moreover, heaven is higher than the Seven Heavens and the Seven Earths.

O God of the mighty beings, we have heard of all Thy marvellous wonders.

[THE DAYS OF CREATION; THE FIRST DAY]

Imagine not, O man, that the first day [of creation] was a day

13

similar to the days of the present time; [Fol. 7a, col. 1] it was not but it was a day which was equal to a period of seven years. And thereat we marvel, saying:

'Thy marvellous works are wonders of craftsmanship',

For Thou art high above the Seven Heavens, and Thou art likewise beneath the Seven Earths.

There is no place wherein Thou art not in Thy Godhead.

There is no limit (*or*, boundary) to Thy sovereign power.

There is no boundary to Thy Lordship.

There is no number (*or*, figure) which can indicate the wealth of Thy wisdom.

There is no measure which representeth the immensity of Thy mercy; [Fol. 7a, col. 2] nay, Thy mercy cooleth Thy wrath, and Thy compassion maketh Thy chastisement to be afar off.

Thou dost not punish man in proportion to his sin, but according to the abundance of Thy mercy.

Who is God except Thyself?

Praise be unto Thee and to the greatness of Thy sovereign power!

Thou didst exist before the world, and Thou will exist for ever, and at this present Thou dost exist.'

[THE SECOND DAY]

And on the Second Day God created a firmament, and a pillar for the wind. For beneath the earth God created four storehouses [Fol. 7b, col. 1] (*or*, chambers) for the winds, with little openings therein, one hundred to the right and one hundred to the left, and also a door. Through all this and through all the doors, we have heard of Thy marvellous works, O Lord.

[THE THIRD DAY]

And on the Third Day God created the sea, and the dry land, and

14

the Garden of 'ÊDÔM in 'ÊDÔM, and every tree which beareth fruit and every tree which doth not; and He created many gardens beyond the East and the West. And among the trees of this Garden were some which resembled white ice (hoar frost?), and some which were like unto a flame of fire [Fol. 7b, col. 2] and some which were like the sun, and emitted rays of light (*or*, sparkled). And the trees of this Garden were not like unto the trees of this world. . . .[1] [The Garden (i.e. Paradise) was situated] above all the high mountains a height of fifteen cubits, [according to] the cubit of the Holy Spirit. And there were in the Garden all kinds of beautiful things which the eye hath not seen, and the ear hath not heard of, and the heart (*or*, mind) of man hath never imagined. These hath God prepared for those who love Him (1 Corinthians ii. 9) [Fol. 8a, col. 1].

[THE FOURTH DAY]

And on the Fourth Day God created the sun, the moon, and the stars. Imagine not that the light of the sun was at that time like unto that which thou seest this day; it was twelve times more brilliant. And the angels said, 'We are unable to go whither Thou dost send us (i.e. the strong light blindeth us); reduce its intensity somewhat.' And God diminished the intensity thereof somewhat, viz. a half; [He withdrew] six parts and [left] six parts. With four [*sic*] parts He made the moon, one part He added to the stars, and one to the waters, and one to the clouds, and one to [Fol. 8a, col. 2] the lightning. Now when thou hearest these things ponder not in doubt over them, saying, 'How is it possible for such things to have happened?' The Scriptures say that on the Fourth Day God made the sun, and moon, and stars; therefore it was even so.

---

[1] Some words seem to have dropped out here. ይእቲ ought to refer to some special tree. I assume that it refers to the Garden.

15

The Army of God consisting of over Five Millions of Angels

And it came to pass that when SEṬNÂ'ÊL perceived the splendour of the sun, and moon, an idea fashioned itself in his mind, saying, 'I will establish my throne above the stars, and I will make myself to be like unto the Most High and Mighty God.' Now as concerning this idea which entered his mind, thou must not imagine that it became completely formed on the fourth day of the week, for this did not happen until the ʿÂREB (Friday) of the second (i.e. following) week. [Fol. 8b, col. 1.]

[THE BATTLE IN HEAVEN]

Thereupon a great battle took place in heaven. And MICHAEL made ready for the battle, and the army of heaven was drawn up in battle array, and God said, 'Come ye, let us see.' And thus saying He inspected the whole of it.

Then SEṬNÂ'ÊL, the most mighty of God's angelic creation, rose up and made war upon Him. And the Most High issued His commands to MICHAEL, and MICHAEL tendered obedience, and rose up [to fight]. And his troops consisted of:

twelve times ten thousand horsemen,

and sixty times ten thousand men of the shield,

and seventy times ten thousand armour-clad warriors [mounted on] horses of fire, [Fol. 8b, col. 2]

and seventy times ten thousand warriors with torches of fire,

and eighty times ten thousand armed with daggers of fire,

and one hundred times ten thousand slingers of stones.

And fifty times ten thousand bearers of axes of fire,

and thirty times ten thousand bearers of crosses of light,

and forty times ten thousand bearers of blazing torches (*or*, lamps).

Seṭnâ'êl's Armies defeated and cast out of Heaven

And this marvellous [force] was in the heavens.

And all the eager combatant angels uttered loud cries and they began to fight, but SEṬNÂ'ÊL broke [their ranks] and they took to flight. And they charged [the enemy] again, and SEṬNÂ'ÊL broke them again and they fled. And when they charged the third time our Lord gave [to them] a cross of light whereon was inscribed [Fol. 9*a*, col. 1] a name (*or*, sign) which read, 'In the Name of the Father, and the Son, and the Holy Spirit'. And when SEṬNÂ'ÊL saw that inscription he was vanquished and MICHAEL cast him down, and he and all his hosts who were banded with him betook themselves to flight.

[DESCRIPTION OF SATAN'S FORM]

The person of SEṬNÂ'ÊL was thus: His height was seventeen hundred cubits, [according to] the angel [cubit]. His head was as large as a great mountain. His mouth was forty cubits [long]. His eyebrows were a journey of three days [in length], and when he wished to cover the 'daughter of his eye' (i.e. the pupil) he was only able to do so after a laborious struggle of seven days. His hand was seventy cubits long, his feet were seven thousand cubits in length, his face was a day's journey in length, and his [Fol. 9*a*, col. 2] phallus was one hundred cubits in length.

Now the angels have phalli, hearken unto [Isaiah vi. 2 and EZEKIEL 1. 12] the prophet, who saith, 'With two of their wings they covered their faces, with two others they covered their feet, with two others they covered their hands, and with two others they covered their phalli.' Know then that the angels have phalli and that among them there is neither male nor female, and that they neither beget nor are brought forth. And the matter which SEṬNÂ'ÊL ejected from his mouth was as large as a mountain to march round which would occupy a day from the morning until the seventh hour, and the spittle which went forth from his mouth was as [the

The Creation of Behemoth and Leviathan

flood of] the JORDAN. Thus terrible in form did God create SEṬNÂ [Fol. 9*b*, col. 1]. And JOB saith unto thee in respect of him, 'There is nothing upon the earth like unto him, and there is no creature who, like him, maketh SHEOL to boil like a cauldron' (Job xli. 22–4).

[DEVILS AND THEIR WORKS]

The devils possessed great power before the coming of our Lord. Some of them smote the eyes of a man with blindness, some of them made his ears deaf, some of them broke his feet, some of them made his hands to wither, some of them made his head to ache, some of them buried him, and some of them made him to be moonstruck and there were those who watched them [balefully]. He watched . . . he feigned to watch. These and all similar sufferings CHRIST brought to an end with His Cross.

Imagine not that I have forgotten thee because of SEṬNÂ'ÊL; [Fol. 9*b*, col. 2] now wait for me (i.e. be patient with me) until I can narrate to thee the story of the creatures which were created on the fifth day.

[THE FIFTH DAY OF CREATION]

On that day were created birds, and fish, and whales, and huge beasts, that is to say, the BĔḤÊMÔT, and LÊWYÂTÂN, the dweller in the waters. And concerning this beast JOB saith, 'It is through them that the abode of the whales which are under the heavens hath been destroyed.' And ENOCH saith, 'There was a day, and the Merciful One was remote from anger.' The great whales are divided into two classes. And there shall be in that day an oath for those who are chosen, and a questioning (*or*, examination) for the sinners. Observe now how men call the beasts which Thou hast created.

[CREATION OF FISH AND BIRDS]

The 'ôRÎT (Pentateuch) saith, (Fol. 10*a*, col. 1] 'And God said, "Let the sea bring forth beasts and birds" (Genesis i. 20)'. Look then

18

The Sun-Birds and the Birds which produce Pearls

and hearken, so that I may narrate unto thee the marvellous story of them which is astounding to hear, how their young grow in them and how they are brought forth, and their creation is more wonderful than that of the birds. There is nothing like unto them under the heavens, and their habitation is nigh unto the Garden (i.e. Paradise). From the time when they were created, there have never been males among these birds, but they all have been females. And then, on the sixth year [after their creation] they ascend into the height of the heavens. In this manner they ascend for three months [of the year], viz. the first month, the third month, and the sixth month, and in these months these birds conceive their young [Fol. 10*a*, col. 2]. And by what are they made to conceive? They conceive by the sun. [Such is] the marvellous statement which we have heard.

[THE BIRDS WHICH PRODUCE PEARLS]

And when that bird hath conceived by the sun, it maketh a hole for itself in the abyss, and it entereth into the sea, in the depth thereof. And remaining therein for seven months it bringeth forth its young in the middle of the eighth month. When it is about to bring forth, first of all it expelleth the birds which are in the left side of its womb, for it carrieth in her womb two kinds [of objects]. On the right side it carrieth pearls of great price, most marvellous gems, and on the left side it carrieth its young. And the name of that bird is KARBÊ-DÎNÊL which is interpreted 'Purest of birds'. And when it bringeth forth it expelleth first of all the birds [Fol. 10*b*, col. 1] which are in its left side. At her first bearing she bringeth forth five young ones, at the second bearing three, and at the third bearing, thirty-nine. And again it beginneth to bring forth the pearls which are in the right side of her womb. At the first bearing she bringeth forth twelve, and at the second bearing seventy, and at the third bearing one splendid pearl. And at this thou wilt be

19

smitten with astonishment, and wilt say, 'Astonishing to me is the work of the Artificer who is the Son of God.'

[THE PEARL FISHERS IN THE EAST]

Then because of the brilliance of the pearls, a mighty beast cometh and swalloweth up the pearls, and he goeth into the sea during the night, and he rendeth in pieces the [other] beasts (i.e. fish) which are on the dry land (i.e. ground). And the birds which were produced in the left side of the womb [of their mother] after having dwelt in [Fol. 10*b*, col. 2] the sea for forty days and forty nights, go forth from the sea, and having developed their wings they fly about. That they produce wings in forty days is a marvellous thing. And in their quest for pearls the merchants come and kill the fish and drag them out [of the sea], and extract the pearls which are in their bellies. And this statement is true and this thing taketh place in the country of the East, [the land of] the men of magic (i.e. the MAGIANS).

[THE SYMBOLISM OF THE BIRD AND THE PEARLS]

Now this bird must be interpreted as the SON. As for the bees they only produce young once—viz. when their queen singeth. We must marvel at this and say, 'Thy marvels are truly told.' This bird which is impregnated by the sun, the sun [Fol. 11*a*, col. 1] is [the sun] which dwelleth in the heavens. The gems of the sea (i.e. the pearls) which were brought forth by the bird are the people who are faithful [Christians]. The twelve pearls which were brought forth at the first birth are the Twelve Apostles; the seventy [which followed] are the Seventy Disciples; and the One Pearl is the One Earth. The Fish is the world. The Five Birds are the Five Books [of MOSES]; the Three Birds are the three Books, JOSHUA, JUDGES, and RUTH, and the Thirty-nine Birds are the thirty-nine Books of the Prophets.

Adam crowned and mounted on an Elephant

[THE SIXTH DAY OF CREATION]

And on the third day our God created the beasts of the desert, and the beasts of the field, and every creature that moveth.

[THE CREATION OF ADAM]

Having created this [world] God said unto His angels [of the earth], 'Bring dust of the earth.' And unto the angels of fire He said, 'Bring *mareb*,' that is to say, fire [Fol. 11*a*, col. 2] in the Syrian language, and they brought it. And to the angels of the waters He said, 'Bring a little water'; and they brought it. And to the angels of the winds He said, 'Bring a little wind'; and they brought it. And He mixed together these four materials and He made of them a perfect man. And the spirit of life which was in His own mouth He breathed upon the face of ADAM. And when He had created him He called him 'ADAM', which is interpreted, 'Thou dost please Me.'

[ADAM IS MOUNTED ON AN ELEPHANT]

Then God said unto His angels, 'This is My image. I have given unto him everything which is lower than Myself [in rank]. Thus saying I have appointed him to be the governor [thereof].' Take four sheep which are in the Garden (i.e. Paradise), and slay them, and smear [Fol. 11*b*, col. 1] thy hand with the blood, and thy right ear, and the fingers of thy right hand, and [the toes of] the right foot. And this shall be a memorial for thy children, and thou shalt become associated with SÛRÂFÊL (i.e. the SERÂPHÎM) in the mysteries.' Then He arrayed ADAM in apparel of light which resembled the flower of the rose, and He bound on his head a magnificent crown one part of which resembled a flame and the other the sun. And he made for him a tunic of light and girded it about his body : and He made a helmet of iron for his skull (*or*, forehead). And God had an elephant brought and He mounted ADAM thereon, and

The Advent of Adam celebrated by Michael and all Angels

He gave him a spear in his hand, and He made sandals of gold for his feet.

Then the hosts of MICHAEL mounted white horses [Fol. 11b, col. 2] and they galloped about. And the SERÂPHÎM carried the Cross of Light and sang songs of rejoicing. And they held:

Five hundred and seventy censers of gold.

Five hundred and seventy censers of silver.

Five hundred and seventy censers of iron.

Five hundred and seventy censers of *sanphêr* (sapphire).

Five hundred and seventy censers of *'îaspîs* (jasper).

Five hundred and seventy censers of the colour of sard.

Five hundred and seventy censers of the colour of *karkedên* (chalcedony).

Five hundred and seventy censers of topaz.

Five hundred and seventy censers of beryl.

Five hundred and seventy censers of *'amatêstînôs* (amethyst).

All these were displayed to make manifest the glory of ADAM, and with one voice they said, 'One is the Father, holy; One is the Son, holy; One is the Holy Spirit, holy. His foot is like unto the stone *sanphêr* (sapphire)—our Good God.' And as concerneth the handicraftsmanship of our God it is, as we have heard, a matter whereat to marvel.

And the man of God [Fol. 12a, col. 1] said, and he spake unto me and said unto me, 'If a man maketh a commemoration of the angels, will God show mercy upon him?'; and he said, 'Yea.' 'And if he maketh a celebration of the Prophets and Apostles [will God show mercy upon him]?' And the angel answered and said unto me, 'Hearken, and I will describe unto thee the power which hath been given unto the angels. There was a certain man of the children of

22

ADAM, and there was never a single occasion on which he did a good deed, and he lived in his iniquity from the very day of his birth. But he possessed one good trait, viz. he celebrated the festival of MICHAEL and he showed compassion on the poor. Then he died, and the devils shouted out cries of joy over him and they said, "[His] soul belongeth to us." [Fol. 12*a*, col. 1.] And they made [their] cry come before God. And God said unto them, "Choose ye now one of two courses. Either let MICHAEL hide him, and ye shall seek him out, or ye shall hide him and MICHAEL shall seek him out, and if he findeth him he shall keep him." And these devils said, "How can we agree to this? For if MICHAEL hideth him we shall never find him, and he will take him to the throne of the Godhead, and how can we find him [there]?" And straightway they said, "We ourselves will hide him." Then these filthy devils hid this man in the abyss of GAHÂNAM (GEHENNA), in the deepest depth thereof. And they said, "Now let MICHAEL search for him, and if he findeth him [Fol. 12*b*, col. 1] he shall go free"; and MICHAEL found him.'

[MICHAEL BRINGS A MAN OUT OF HELL]

And MICHAEL said, 'Get ye gone and depart ye from this place.' And he went into SHEOL and descended into the depths thereof and he did not find the man he was seeking. And on the first occasion he brought out on his wings sixty thousand [souls], and similarly with [each of] his six wings he brought out sixty thousand [souls]. And on the second occasion he brought out [a like number] but he did not find the man he was seeking. And he penetrated the depths of hell laboriously a third time, and he raked GAHÂNAM to pieces and brought out that man. And the number of those [souls] who through that man escaped from SHEOL was five hundred and forty-six thousand. And some of these were heathen. And the angels said, 'This thing is terrifying.'

The Supreme Efficiency of Baptism

And our Lord saith in the Gospel, 'He who believeth and who is baptized [Fol. 12b, col. 2] shall be saved, but he who believeth not shall be damned' (Mark xvi. 16). How then was it possible for these [souls] to escape? And thee, O son of man, hast thou heard that some of the heathen have been saved? [No doubt thou hast], but they did not enter the Garden (Paradise) without being baptized, for MICHAEL baptized them, and they shone with splendour like the sun. And the Holy Abbâ (Father) marvelled, and said, 'AMÂNÛ'ÊL hath the power to do everything.' And again GABRIEL answered and said, 'I marvel at the children of men. They do not reward him that hath done good to them; only here and there can a few be found who do.'

[HOW SATAN ENTERED PARADISE; THE BIRDS REFUSE TO HELP HIM]

Now concerning SEṬNÂ. Do not imagine that I have forgotten to speak unto thee concerning SEṬNÂ. In the first place he schemed with guile and came to the Garden so that he might seduce [Fol. 13a, col. 1] ADAM. And before all [the other birds] he found a certain white bird the name of which is ''ARZEL', and SEṬNÂ said unto him, 'Wilt thou do what I shall say unto thee.' And the bird said, 'What [is that]?' And SEṬNÂ said unto him, 'Take me and bring me to ḤÊWÂ (EVE)'. And the bird said unto him, 'I will not.' And SEṬNÂ departed from him and passed onwards and found a green bird the name of which is 'BEREL'. And SEṬNÂ said unto him, 'Take me and bring me to ḤÊWÂ (EVE).' And the bird made no reply [but] refused. And again he found a bird the whole plumage of which was red, and he said unto it, 'Take me and bring me to ḤÊWÂ.' And the bird refused; and all the birds of every kind whatsoever refused likewise.

[HOW SATAN ENTERED PARADISE; THE ANIMALS REFUSE TO HELP HIM]

Then SEṬNÂ went to the animals. And before all [the other

beasts] he met a huge animal the name of which is 'FALFAL' which in the ḤABASHÎ (i.e. Ethiopian or Abyssinian) language is called 'ḤARMÂZ' rhinoceros [Fol. 13*a*, col. 2], and with him there was also a lion. [And he said unto] the two of them, 'Take ye me and bring ye me to ḤÊWÂ.' And they said unto him, 'We will not,' and they refused. And again he met a ferocious animal the name of which was 'YEBÊRA', which in the ḤABASHÎ language is called 'NAMER' (i.e. tiger, *or* leopard), and he said unto him, 'Take me and bring me to ḤÊWÂ'; and he refused. And SEṬNÂ passed on, and again he met a beast with a filthy nature, the name of which was called 'FENFENET', which in the ḤABASHÎ language is called 'ZE'EB' (i.e. hyaena), and he refused [to take him to ḤÊWÂ]. Then SEṬNÂ met a black animal the name of which was 'MAGDEL' that is to say, 'DEB' (i.e. the black bear); and he likewise refused [to take SEṬNÂ to ḤÊWÂ]. And again he met an animal, the ḤARÂWĔYÂ, that is to say 'MAFELES' (i.e. the wild boar) which hath terrible tusks. And he hurled himself on SEṬNÂ who fled. And SEṬNÂ met [another] animal, which is called 'SEREG'; he is cloud-coloured, and his name is 'KARÂYÛ(?) MAḲÂBER' (i.e. digger of graves). At the present time he lives in a lake (*or* river, *or* canal). [Fol. 13*b*, col. 1.] And SEṬNÂ said unto him, 'Take me and bring me to ḤÊWÂ'; and the beast refused. And again SEṬNÂ met another beast the name of which was 'TAMAN' in the ḤABASHÎ language; at first [sight] he resembles a young camel. And SEṬNÂ said unto him, 'Take me and bring me to ḤÊWÂ'; and the beast said unto him, 'I will do so.'

[SATAN ENTERS PARADISE ON THE BACK OF A CAMEL]

And SEṬNÂ mounted on the body of the beast came and stood before ḤÊWÂ, and he said unto her, 'What commands hath your God given unto you?' And she said unto him, 'He hath said unto us, From every tree which is in the Garden, eat ye, but of one tree ye shall not eat.' And through the mouth of the serpent SEṬNÂ said unto her, 'He hath spoken unto you in this wise so that ye may not become God even like Himself.' And EVE took [fruit from that tree] and ate thereof and gave it to her husband; and the two of them ate together.

[THE FORBIDDEN TREE]

And the name of [Fol. 13*b*, col. 2] that tree whereof ADAM and EVE ate is 'SEZEN' that is to say 'SENDÂLÊ' (i.e. the 'flour of wheat') in the 'AG'ÂZÎ (Ethiopian) language. Thou must not imagine that this tree was like unto a tree of this world, or like an ear of wheat of this world, for the tree was majestic in its appearance, and one ear of wheat contained one hundred and fifty thousand grains. And the trees which were round about it were [four], one on the east, one on the west, one on the north, and one on the south—even as our Lord said to the CHERÛBHÎM and the SERÂPHÎM, 'Keep watch over the Tree of Life which turneth round(?),' that is to say which returneth to ADAM. And He also said, 'ADAM hath become like unto one of us; peradventure he will take hold of it, and eat [of the fruit] of the Tree of the Garden, and live for ever' (Genesis iii. 23).

[THE TREE OF LIFE SYMBOLIC OF CHRIST]

And that [Tree of Life] is the Body of Christ [Fol. 14*a*, col. 1] which none of the SERÂPHÎM touch without reverent awe. And when ADAM was seduced and ate of the tree it was the third hour of the day. And as ADAM made the tree to suffer, even so our Lord suffered on the Cross, and before He was hung thereon PILATE scourged Him with forty stripes.

[THE ANGELS BECOME MEN AND COMMIT SIN]

Let us come back once again to the people of the Flood. And in those days the Watchers (i.e. angels) came down from heaven, and

The Angels who taught Men the Arts and Crafts

after they had put on the flesh (or, bodies) of men, the madness of sin seized them, and they were thrust aside from the mysteries which they had seen in heaven.

And this number, ⅄ ⅄ is to be interpreted ⅌ i.e. 100 × 100 or 10,000, and their young children are to be interpreted ⅍⅍ i.e. 70 × 70 or 4,900.

[THE OCCUPATIONS OF THE ANGELS ON EARTH (?)]

First of all 'AKARÊ who carrieth [Fol. 14a, col. 2] in his eyes four 'entalâm—and this [is] the figure four:

and PIPIRÔS runneth with the sun;

and RÛRÎDÊ who smasheth the mountains;

and the inventor of the circle ZAR'ÊL, which is the moon (or, month);

and PÎNÊNÊ who showed [men] the running (racing) of horses;

and GÂLÊ showed [men] how to hold the gadab, that is to say the galab (fish-hook) as it is interpreted in the Abyssinian language;

and TÎGANA showed [men] how to make the shield;

and HÔRÊRÎ taught [men] the harp;

and YUEBÊ taught [men] how to work in iron;

and MÊGÊA taught [men] how to ride the horse;

and NEGÔDÎ showed [men] springs of [mineral] waters and healed the sick [therewith], and the [proper] hour (or, season) when they would benefit the sick man; and one of them wished to snatch away everything which the children of CAIN had taken. He took fifty sâdâla that is to say, fifty 'entalâm [Fol. 14b, col. 1], which he carried away in his right hand.

O this thing hard [to understand]—the gift of Him Who created both the weak and the strong!

And GARGÊ showed [men the pattern of] the corn-grinder;

and SÊTÊR showed [men] how to knead dough;

The Angels who taught Men the Arts and Crafts

and GÎMÊR [showed men] how to extract food from [raw] plasma;
and ZÂRÊ showed [men] how to milk animals;
and ḤEGGÊ showed [men] how to work in wood and make a roof
  for the house;
and ṬENṬÔREB-'AREB(?) showed [men how to make] the door;
and SÊPHÊR showed [men] how to boil milk (?);
and HALÊGÊ showed [men] carving (or, sculpture);
and HÊDER showed [men] how to make the tree flourish;
and SÎNÔ showed [men] how to build;
and TÔF showed [men] how to burn clay (or, mud, i.e. how to
  make pottery);
and 'ARṬÔRBEGÂS showed [men how to make] cutting tools;
and ṢBÊDÊGUÂZ showed [men] stibium(?) (eye-paint);
and ZÂRÊ showed [men] [Fol. 14b, col. 2] how to make must (or,
  wine);
and BÊTÊNÊLÂDÂS showed [men] the bread oven;
and NÂFÎL showed [men] the planting [of trees];
and YÂRBEḤ showed [men] how to saw up wood;
and 'ELYÔ showed [men] how to dance;
and PHENÊMÛS showed [men] architecture and writing;
and 'EGÂLÊMÛN showed [men how to make] yokes for cattle and
  the chariot-pole;
and KUERES showed [men how to make] the body of the chariot
  and the whip (or, goad);
and 'AKÔR showed [men how to make] brass;
And there were among them some who taught [men] to work the
cedar and the willow. And WASAG and 'ABÊRGEYÂ, whose heads
shone in the clouds, showed [men] all these things; they it was who
taught men to play ṬÂBAT. And [Fol. 15a, col. 1] NÊR and ZABÊRÊNÎ-
GUED taught them to play 'AFÂWEMÂ, and 'AKÎS taught them the
Circus.

Adulteries and Fornications brought about the Flood

[MEN'S EVIL LIVES CAUSED THE FLOOD]

Now, it was through these men that the waters of the Flood came upon the earth; seven in the heavens, and seventy on the earth. Of great [magnitude] were the outpourings of water which were set loose in those days! Evil had multiplied and had filled the earth. Whoredom had magnified itself and even the four-footed beasts went mad. Neither a father nor his son [respected each other], for no son considered his father, and no father his son. Men consorted with the beasts. Even the earth complained and uttered lamentations.

[THE DESTRUCTION OF THE GIANTS AND THE FLOOD]

And the Creator said concerning them: 'Hold [thy] peace. Mine eye seeth them, and Mine ear hath heard them, and My longsuffering hath made Me silent in respect of them.' [Fol. 15a, col. 2.] And in those days harlotry had increased to such an extent that it merited the taking of the vengeance which God had not hitherto commanded.[1] And in those days He took vengeance on the giants and a voice went forth which said, 'Kill ye each other with the sword.' And the waters of the Flood rose and swallowed up their bodies as far as their breasts, and they hacked off their heads with the sword. And in those days NOAH and his sons clung to righteous dealing and they were saved from destruction.

[THE BUILDING OF THE TOWER OF BABEL]

Subsequently the men who followed after them (i.e. their progeny) did not keep righteous dealing, and they began to build a tower (or, fortress). And during the building of the same they came [to a height] where they heard the sound of the angels. And God said, 'Come ye, let us go down and see the children of men [Fol. 15b, col. 1],

[1] i.e. it was so great that God could not possibly refrain any longer from taking vengeance.

29

and what they have been doing. For all their labour is in vain and unprofitable, and their words also are vain and unprofitable.' And God overturned the tower and seventy thousand [men] perished through the combustion (*or*, lightning) of the earth and the dust, without reckoning women and children. And at that time every man had the same speech (*or*, language); and it was changed forthwith, and they were unable to hold converse with each other. And they spread abroad in their various countries and were dispersed.

[THE LANGUAGES OF THE CHILDREN OF SHEM]

'ARÎ	'AZÎ	SÂRÎ	'EBRÎ	FÎLÎ
KÊLÎ	HÊNÎ	SÊNÎ	'A'ÊYUI	TAKÊLÎ
NÔGÎ	ḲÊNÎ	MÊLYÂRÎ	KAKĔLÎ	MÂTÎ
LÊMÎ	ḤEḤENÎ	YÊYÊNÎ	ḲEṬÊṬÎ	LÊMÊMÎ
'ASÊRÎ	TÔRÎ	MÔDÎ		

And their alphabets are eight.

'ÔRÎ means ARAB, just as thou callest ''ÔRÎTA' those who remain [Fol. 15*b*, col. 2].

And SÊRÎ they call ZAMÎN, and 'ÔRÎ they call HEBREWS;
and FÎRÎ means FÂRS;
and KÊLÎ means the KALADÂWÎYÂN;
and HÊNÎ means the HÊNÔSÂWÎYÂN;
and SÊRÎ means the 'ASÊRÂWÎYÂN, that is the son of SHEM;
and TEKÛLÎ means TEKÛN;
and NÔGÎ means the NÂGÊBÂWÎYÂN;
and ḲANÊ means the ḲANÂWÎYÂN;
and MÊLÎ means the MÊLÂWÎYÂN;
and YÂRÊ means the YÂRÊMÂWÎYÂN;
and KĔKĔMÎ means the KANÂNÂWÎYÂN;
and MÂTÎ means the MÂTÊNÂN;
and LÊMÂ means the LÊMÂWÎYÂN;

30

and ḤENNÎ means the ḤENÔTÂWÎYÂN;
and SEMDÎ means the SEMDÂWÎYÂN;
and YÊYÊNÎ means the YÔNÂNÂWÎYÂN;
and KÊṬÊṬÎ means the KEṬÊWÔN;
and LÊMÊMÎ means the LÊMÂWÎYÂN;
and SÔRÎ means the SÔRÊYÂWÎYÂN;
and MÔṢÎ means the MÔSÂWÎYÂN.

These are the nations of SEM, each according to their tribes, [Fol. 16a, col. 1] and their languages.

[THE LANGUAGES OF THE CHILDREN OF HÂM]

And as concerning the children of HÂM the following are their languages:

ḲEBṬÎ	GEBEṢ	ḤABASÎ	NÔZAZÎ	DÊNKÎL
DÊMÊSÂWÎ	'ENZÎ	'ENDERÎ	SÛLÎ	DÎDÛBÎ
KANÎ	MANBARÎ	TARÎBNÎ	ḲÔRÎ	DÛRÎ
MÎKÎ	KUE'ZÎ	HÊMÎ	LÊBÎ	SÊRÊWÎ
LÊZÎ				

ḲEBṬÎ means COPTIC, and GEBEṢ means EGYPTIAN.

And the ḤABASÎ are the people of TEGRÊ;

and the NÔBÎ are the NUBIANS;

and FÊSÎ means the 'AELÔPHELÎ (PHILISTINES?);

and the ZÂRÎ are the ZARÂWÎYÂN, the people who dwell in front of the mountains of fire;

and the LÎBÂ (LYBIANS?) [dwell] to the west of them.

And the BÂLÎ live in a place where a woman reigneth, to the east of YÂPHÊT. Now as concerneth this woman who reigneth, when [Fol. 16a, col. 2] [the end of] her days draweth nigh the SATANS seize her, and they make another woman queen in her stead. In this wise they rule over that country for ever.

And zêzî means the zâguâ;

and zâhî means sêhô;

and mesî means mêks;

and ḥazî means ḥazô;

and nâkî means the dankêlen, and to the west of them are the sêmî.

And sêwî means shoa;

and 'enzî means 'angôt;

and 'enderî means sel'edân;

and sôrî means the army of sel'edân and dêdûbî their brothers;

and kônî means kânâ'an;

and manbarî means manbartâ and dêrî and 'endertâ;

and bûnî means the beguenâ.

And these are not all the children of hâm. Those of hâm are: dûrî which means dabr.

mâkî, malakî, and kue'ez mean kue'ên.

hâmî means ḥam.

And [Fol. 16*b*, col. 1] lêbî means lîbân;

and sôrî means sîrê;

and lêgî, lagô means the danṣewân;

And wakûrî means the waḳaret, the cutters of stones of great price when solomon made the Sanctuary.

These are the habitations and the languages of the children of hâm; and the number of their languages are thirty.

[THE NAMES OF THE LANGUAGES OF THE CHILDREN OF JAPHET]

RÔMÊN	'APHENGÊN	'AṬERNÎ	'APHLEKNÎ
NÂNÎ	KÂLANÎ	'ARÎ	YESÎ
YENÎ	DÎBÎKUERÎ	YÂDÎ	PÎRÎ
MÂRÎ	SÊṬI	BÂRÎ	NÂRÎ

These are the children of JAPHET according to their tribes.

Abraham the Monotheist

[THE HISTORY OF ABRAHAM; HIS BIRTH]

And at a subsequent period ABRAHAM the believer was famous. On the day of his birth the house shone with a bright light. Very many things (*or*, persons) fell down, [Fol. 16*b*, col. 2] and there was an outcry in a mighty voice, which said, 'Woe is me! Woe is me! There hath just been born him that shall crush my Kingdom to dust.' And [he who uttered] the voice wept, and described events which would take place, and said, 'This is he who shall overturn my habitation.'

And among [those present] there were some who said, 'Kill this child forthwith'; and those who said this knew full well that [divine] grace would be given to ABRAHAM. And God poured compassion into the heart [of the father of] ABRAHAM, and he said unto the SATANS [who advised him thus]: 'Whence come ye, ye who say unto me that I must kill my child, an act pleasing to God?' And he reared the child.

[ABRAHAM'S FIRST TALK WITH GOD]

And at the beginning of the seventh month ABRAHAM went forth by night and he saw the moon and the stars, and he said, '[Who art] Thou God who [Fol. 17*a*, col. 1] hast created these?' And straightway God said unto him, 'I am the God of thy Fathers. I will make thee to be justified and I will magnify thee.' And he gave him the covenant of the Law and an ordinance (*or*, rules for social life).

[CIRCUMCISION OF ABRAHAM]

And ABRAHAM was circumcised by the hand of GABRIEL, and MICHAEL who assisted him. And the man of God said, 'This mysterious matter is astounding, and no one among men hath discovered it.' And the angel said unto me, 'God did not tell MOSES that ABRAHAM had been circumcised by the hands of angels. And He

33   F

told it neither to His Prophets nor His Apostles. Glory and praise be unto Him who revealeth His hidden things unto whomsoever He pleaseth. Even as He Himself saith, 'My gold [Fol. 17a, col. 2] I give to him to whom I wish to give it. And there is no one who shall say unto me, This [man] Thou hast made to suffer, and this [man] Thou hast made happy; this [man] Thou hast made wealthy and this [man] Thou hast reduced to beggary.'

What God showed by ABRAHAM was the whole ordinance of righteousness: faith [came] by ABRAHAM, and the ordinance (i.e. rules of life) by ABRAHAM. And in this we may marvel that the whole of the Law of our God abideth for ever, and is never abrogated, even as ENOCH saith: 'I saw fourteen trees from which the leaves had not been stripped. And all the [other] trees were withered and stripped of their leaves.' And what do these fourteen trees of which ENOCH speaketh symbolize? saith Abbâ BAKHAYLA MÎKÂ'ÊL. And the Holy Ghost saith(?), '[They symbolize] the Ten Words of the 'ôRÎT, the Covenant of NOAH, the Circumcision of the Fathers, the Priesthood of MELCHISEDEK, and the Baptism of JOHN.

[GOD'S SPEECH TO ABRAHAM]

But God told [Fol. 17b, col. 1] ABRAHAM when he made an offering to Him [and] He informed him that [he] should go down into EGYPT, a stranger, [and] that he should be in a foreign land and that he should serve them (i.e. the EGYPTIANS) for twelve years. And this took place because SÂRÂ laughed and did not believe the word of God. And if MOSES had not been saved [from drowning] the HEBREWS would never have gone up out from the sea [of reeds]. And in the New Law it saith, 'If our Lord had not been saved from HÊRÔDES the people would never have gone up out from the sea of sin.'

Michael brought the Hebrews out of Egypt

[SAINT MICHAEL LED THE MAGI AND BROUGHT THE ISRAELITES SAFELY
THROUGH THE RED SEA]

And thou must not imagine that the MAGI came [to BETHLEHEM] after [CHRIST] was born, or that they rose up from their country two years before [Fol. 17*b*, col. 2] our Lord was born [of their own prompting], for MICHAEL in the form of the Star guided them. And it was he who brought out the HEBREWS [from EGYPT]. For when he smote the cloud there was rain. And the angels of the clouds pressed out the water and made it to fall [into the sea], and through the rain one thousand soldiers died. Then for three days and three nights there was bitter (*or*, freezing) cold, and one thousand men died through the cold. And the HEBREWS remained in the water three days and three nights, and then monsters of the water (*or*, sea) went forth and killed the EGYPTIANS. Some of these monsters were like lions, and some like leopards, and some like bears, and some like serpents (*or*, boa-constrictors) [Fol. 18*a*, col. 1]. And they all uttered horrible noises and the EGYPTIANS were terror-stricken, and before they reached the sea these monsters rushed to meet them.

[PHARAOH AND HIS HORSE]

And it is because of this that the Teacher of the Wise saith, 'Through the noises of the wild beasts, which uttered terrifying cries as they came to attack them, the EGYPTIANS were smitten with fright. The horse of PHARAOH wished to march on dry land, but MOSES said, 'We praise and glorify Him. Let Him who is praised and glorious be praised and glorified!', whereupon the horse of PHARAOH leaped up into the air to a height of fifteen cubits (i.e. 22½ or 30 feet). When the people saw the leap of PHARAOH's horse they were terrified. And MOSES cursed the horse and forthwith there remained to the horse only three-ninths of his original strength. And everything which belonged to PHARAOH sank into the water and descended into SHEOL.

And [Fol. 18a, col. 2] relating to this event, EZEKIEL saith: 'The abyss groaneth and he hath descended into SHEOL.' [The words] 'the abyss groaneth' refer to the sea which for seven days and seven nights wept like a child.

[THE MARVELLOUS THINGS WROUGHT BY GOD]

[Such are] Thy marvels, O Lord, and behold, we have heard them all with our ears (Psalm xliii. 1, 2). Thy marvels, O Lord, are tremendous, and behold, the Holy Word is Thine own. Thy throne is founded on integrity and the roof thereof [resteth] on righteousness. Before the throne is a whirlwind and a blazing fire, which the wind penetrateth throughout, and surroundeth each of the four sides for a distance of ten thousand [cubits]. And the wind is like unto a flame of fire, and nothing (or, no one) can see it except the Eye of God. And that wind beareth along the Chariot of the CHERÛBHÎM.

[THE NUMBER SEVEN]

[Fol. 18b, col. 1] And there is the Lake (or, Sea) of Fire and the number thereof is seven. [There are] seven abysses (or, seas?) of light, seven stars of brilliant light, the seven monstrances of light, the seven clouds of light, the seven grapes (vines?) of the waters, the seven stones of ice, and the seven mountains of light which ENOCH, the son of YÂRÊD, saw. And he heard the words of the angels, and thus the angels taught him.

[THE GENEALOGY OF THE FATHERS]

Here is the genealogy of the Patriarchs. ABRAHAM begot ISAAC, and ISAAC begot JACOB, and JACOB begot twelve Patriarchs. And these envied JOSEPH and sold him, and before they sold him they said, 'Let us kill him.' And REUBEN prevented them and said unto them, 'Let that [act] be far from us. [Fol. 18b, col. 2] We will not kill him.' And he saved him, and because he had saved him his sin was done away.

[JOSEPH FLIES TO A TREE FOR SAFETY]

JOSEPH, having taken shelter under a tree, the tree said unto him, 'Thy brethren are taking counsel together to kill thee.' And JOSEPH was afraid and fled [from the tree], and he wandered about in the desert for three days and three nights and he was ahungered. And a stone said unto him, 'Eat me for I shall become bread.' And JOSEPH ate the stone and gave thanks to his Creator; and some water came forth from that bread. And he removed himself a short distance from that place, and he met a snarer of partridges, who said unto him, 'Whence comest thou?' And JOSEPH said unto him, 'I am hiding myself from the face[s] of my brethren, because of [my] fear of them.' And the snarer of partridges gave him one of the partridges which he had caught in his net. And on the seventh day his brethren found him and they sold him into a remote(?) country [Fol. 19a, col. 1].

[JOSEPH IS NOT FORSAKEN BY GOD]

Now in this state of things the graciousness of God did not forsake him. What then are we to say, [O] man, if the graciousness of God was with him? Through a false charge he was cast into prison, and here God did not forsake him, and His graciousness was with him. Even as SOLOMON saith, 'In the prison house it did not forsake him.' The king appointed him [with the titles of] ''ÊL, 'ÊL', and ''ABRÎR' (Genesis xli. 40) which are interpreted 'Hear, hear' (i.e. obey). Other facts concerning the history of JOSEPH are written in the 'ÔRÎT (Pentateuch).

[THE ISRAELITES IN EGYPT]

Now the ISRAELITES went down into EGYPT, and the EGYPTIANS

37

persecuted them. And in those days PÎNÂḤAS, the son of PHÂNÎKA, flourished and the name of his wife was RÂḤÊL. And whilst they were making bricks, through the great severity of the labour the pangs of childbirth came upon her and she had a miscarriage—now there were twins in her womb—and she cried out and said, 'Hast Thou forgotten Thy [Fol. 19*a*, col. 2] people, [O] God of ISRAEL?' Thereupon God came down on Mount SÎNÂ, and said, 'Assuredly I have seen the tribulation of My people, and I have heard their cry and I have come down to deliver them' (Exodus xi. 7).

[MOSES AND THE LAMB]

And MOSES was obedient to his Lord, and this is the ordinance which God laid upon the children of ISRAEL in the land of EGYPT. And He said unto them, 'Let every man take a lamb in the first month, on the tenth day thereof, and it shall be guarded by you until the fourteenth day' (Exodus xii. 3, 6). And as concerning what He saith, He spake prophetically, and showed forth the coming of our Lord in the last days. The head of the lamb is the Divine Word, our Lord JESUS CHRIST, and his hands (i.e. paws) are the Prophets from ADAM to ABRAHAM. His feet [Fol. 19*b*, col. 1] on the left side indicate the Prophets from MOSES to ELIAS, and his hands on the right side indicate the Prophets from SAMUEL to JEREMIAH. The fingers of his hands and feet are the sons of the Prophets, and his skin is the gift of the Holy Spirit which warmeth the peoples to life; even as SOLOMON saith, 'If two people sleep [side by side] they kindle warmth in each other', the two persons being the Old and the New Law. And his eyes are the Apostles for the eye of their light [illuminateth] the whole world. And the hearing of his ears are PETER and PAUL. And the breathing of his two nostrils is the fervour of the faith of the Martyrs. His bowels are the voice (*or*, word) of the Scriptures, and his belly are the priesthood, the Faith, love [Fol.

19*b*, col. 2] baptism, and the Offering. The two horns of the lamb and his bone which is not broken [symbolize] the body (*or*, flesh) of MARY whom no man hath touched. It is because of this that ISAIAH saith, 'A crushed reed he breaketh not, and the smouldering rag of linen he extinguisheth not' (Isaiah xlii. 3). The 'crushed reed' of which he speaketh is the body of ADAM which was not broken on the Cross, and the 'rag of linen' of which he speaketh is the Offering (*or*, Sacrifice) of the nations (Gentiles?), the ritual of which shall never be blotted out.

[GOD'S COMMAND TO MOSES CONCERNING THE TABERNACLE]

And God said unto MOSES: 'When thou hast completed the tabernacle after the following manner thou shalt appoint it, since I Myself have made thee governor thereof.' Then He said unto him, 'Select an ox from among the oxen (*or*, cattle), and fat sheep, and unleavened bread soaked in oil, and fine flour of wheat, and lay them on a piece of basket work [Fol. 20*a*, col. 1]. And thou shalt take them to AARON and his two sons at the door of the tabernacle of testimony, and thou shalt wash them with water. And the apparel of AARON shall be a tunic (*or*, short shirt), and on his head covering shall be a band of gold. This is the ordinance for their apparel; they shall be girded with a belt and shall wear a turban (Leviticus viii. 1–10).

[THE SYMBOLISM OF THE PRECEDING PARAGRAPH EXPLAINED]

Here is the spiritual interpretation [of the preceding paragraph]. When He saith 'ox,' He meaneth ADAM, even as ENOCH saith, 'A white ox went forth, from his flank went forth a calf (*or*, lamb).' Now what ENOCH saith unto thee hath reference to [the creation of] EVE. The horns of the altar which are drenched with the blood of the ox are the Prophets who have received [the gift of] prophecy.

The Symbolism of the Ox and the Rams

And when He speaketh of the fat of the belly of the ox, He meaneth the priesthood. And his neck and breast and his two kidneys are ABRAHAM, ISAAC, and JACOB [Fol. 20a, col. 2].

And when He saith, 'Thou shalt burn the ox outside, having brought him out from the camp' [know] that the ox is the second ADAM, that is to say CHRIST Who died outside the camp, even as the Gospel saith, 'They brought Him outside the camp and took Him to crucify Him' (John xix. 20). Moreover, ADAM, the father of the world [of men], went forth from the Garden (Paradise) and was burnt with fire. Thou must not imagine that he was consumed entirely like those of his sons and his children who were sinners. The Prophets dwelt in SHEOL, but SHEOL did not burn them up. And to them ADAM was an abyss of water, for to the man who hath not committed sin SHEOL becometh an abyss of mercy. And it is because of this that DAVID saith, 'From out of the abyss of the earth Thou hast brought me again' [Fol. 20b, col. 1].

[THE TWO RAMS]

And the second ram of which He speaketh is MOSES. This ram, which hath never been found perfect, is the offering (or, sacrifice) of ISRAEL. And as concerning their offerings (or, sacrifices) and their Prophets none hath been found perfect, but all of them are made perfect by the Gospel. The third ram, which is perfect, is our Lord, Who is the completion of what is incomplete. The breast of the ram of which he speaketh is that part whereon grow the teats, and men call it 'Samsam'.

[THE CONSECRATION OF THE LEVITES]

I will now describe unto thee the anointing (or, consecration) of the LEVITES. And the angel said, As the LEVITES are consecrated with bread, even so are the priests consecrated with bread when the

PÂPÂS ordaineth them. When they take the bread [Fol. 20*b*, col. 2] they bear it on the paten and perform what is appointed for them. Then, in divers ways (*or*, aspects) they see the Mystery. Some see it as bread purely and simply, and some like a flame of fire, and to some it hath the form of an ear of wheat. And the man on hearing this description of the Mystery cried, 'Thou art able [to do] everything, and there is nothing which is too hard for Thee [to do]', even as SOLOMON saith, 'From olden time Thou hast been able to make Thyself to resemble everything.' Now although the priests are ordained [to perform] everything, they do not all with strict exactness devote themselves to the observation of the Mystery. There are some priests who pass their whole day in administering the Offering (*or*, Sacrifice), and they see the Lamb being slain on the paten, and there are others who officiate in the customary manner, without [Fol. 21*a*, col. 1] seeing the Lamb being sacrificed. And, even as the Apostles say, 'They are all of equal rank by their ordination, but their portions (i.e. their spiritual rewards) are not equal.' And Christian people receive [the Mysteries] with one single Spirit and one single Faith (*or*, Belief). Now on those men who say in the humility of their hearts, 'I am unworthy to put on the garb of the priesthood', doth God direct His vision. It is very meet and right for a man to adopt humility; there are some whose understanding hath not been opened since they were baptized.

Now, as the tips of all the fingers of AARON and his sons were anointed, in like manner doth the Holy Spirit anoint the end of the right hand and the edge of the right ear of the priests when they are ordained. And this taketh place by means of a marvellous sign which is invisible to the eye [of the spectator] [Fol. 21*a*, col. 2]. In the case of deacons it is the tip of the left hand which [is anointed by the Holy Spirit]. This thou shalt not make known to ordinary men, but only to those who are wise and understanding. If thou makest this known unto all men thou shalt not have a portion in the kingdom of the heavens. This did the angel who was sent unto me say unto me.

[THE SOUL]

Now as concerneth the soul, it is without power, because of that which man knoweth not; for the mortal mind is darkened.

[THE BASKET]

The sacrificial basket is to be interpreted as the Christians, for the Body of our Lord is buried in us. And when we die He crieth out, and saith, 'Abbâ, and My Father by the Holy Ghost'. And [God] saith unto the soul, 'O soul, I have mercy on thee because thou hast eaten the flesh (*or*, Body) of My Son.'

[THE MORTAL BODY]

And the body (*or*, flesh) [Fol. 21*b*, col. 1] which becometh dust in the grave do the angels keep guard over. And the Book saith, 'Many shall rise up from the dust of the earth through the burning up of the earth.' And our Lord Himself keepeth guard over the bones of the righteous. And it is because of this that DANIEL saith, 'MICHAEL, the great angel, shall rise up for the children of the people. And through him there shall be a great tribulation the like of which hath never been since the world was created.' By MICHAEL is to be understood an astounding matter (*or*, thing). And the words which DANIEL saith mean the Son Who rose up on the Cross. And among the men who have lived in olden time and those who shall live in time to come, there is none who suffered or shall suffer like our Lord. And Him we worship equally with His Father and the Holy Ghost.

[THE HOLY TABERNACLE]

Let us return now [Fol. 21*b*, col. 2] to our discourse on the holy

The Tabernacle of Moses

Tabernacle. Here are the words wherewith he (i.e. MOSES) commanded the children of ISRAEL. And he ordered them to bring of
their possessions silver, and cloths, and hyacinth, and purple-red,
and thick cloth, and byssus, and hair of the goat, and dressed skins
of sheep, and hides of the *mâḥan*. Now the hide of the sheep
mâḥan means red leather. And *maṣâsît*, that is to say *sârâk*, meaneth
red (*or*, pink) and is what the LEVITES wear on their feet. And what
MOSES commanded was carried out faithfully.

[THE TREE, ETC.]

When he (i.e. MOSES) speaketh of the tree which never rotteth,
and the name of which is *sôm*, he referreth to the black tree which
is called in GĔ'ĔZ *zôpê* (i.e. ebony). And the *pôdêrê* (i.e. tunic), which
is a white garment, symbolizeth the Holy Ghost. And *papîra* is the
tail of a white ox [Fol. 22*a*, col. 1] which [the priest used] to drive
away small insects (i.e. as a fly whisk). The *mêlâk* which is cleaner
than every other cloth, hath a white colour, and it must be interpreted
by ADAM.

[THE TABERNACLE—*continued*]

Now the pillars of the Tabernacle of which he (i.e. MOSES) speaketh
were of gold: gold symbolizes the Prophets and silver the Apostles.
And the cross-bars of the pillar, and their capitals and bases, and
the tools (?), and the struts of the pillars above and below, and their
pediments were to be of brass. And the [ornaments] which they made
for the vestments of AARON they made of gold. And they made for
it four rows of stones, and they engraved thereon the names of the
children of ISRAEL, and they sealed with each one of these names.

[THE SYMBOLISM OF THE ABOVE PARAGRAPH EXPLAINED]

The four [rows of] stones are to be interpreted by the Four
Gospels; and the twelve names [of the children of] ISRAEL by the

43

Twelve Apostles [Fol. 22*a*, col. 2], even as SOLOMON saith, 'The glory of the Fathers (Patriarchs) is engraved on the four rows of stones; on the vestment of the [high] priest is all the world.' And when SOLOMON said this he did so because the [high] priest commemorateth the whole world when he offereth up incense.

[THE BREASTPLATE]

The vestment called 'LÔGYÔN' (i.e. λογεῖον) is as long as it is broad, and the colour of this vestment which he (i.e. MOSES) calls 'LÔGYÔN' resembleth that of the sea. It is as broad as it is long and is the most glorious of all the vestments of the [high] priest. And AARON and his sons only wore it on days of the greatest festivals. But the vestment ĶÂS (loin-cloth), and the mitre, and the vestment 'AGÊ, which was dark in colour, they put on when cleansing or when they were cooking the flesh [offering]. And he put on the mitre always for this ordinance(?).

[THE AREAS (*or,* ENCLOSURES)]

[Fol. 22*b*, col. 1] As concerneth the areas (*or,* enclosures) the length of each was four cubits and one palm breadth. And they made a purple-coloured and liver-coloured veil (*or,* curtain). And on it they made figures of the CHERÛBHÎM and they placed it between four pillars of wood which never decayeth plated with gold, and the feet (*or,* bases) were of gold. The door of the Tabernacle was made of worked purple, and on it they made figures of the CHERÛBHÎM of the creation(?) (*feṭerat*). Now the *feṭerat* are two sets of thrones facing(?) the four sides. Of these, one has the face of a man, and one the face of a beast, and one the face of an ox, and one the face of a lion. And the face of a man depicteth a man, and the face of the lion the lions, and the face of the eagle, which is also depicted, figureth the birds, and the face of the beast the beasts. From the wings [of the CHERÛ-

44

BHÎM] descendeth the dew of mercy [Fol. 22*b*, col. 2] on those who ask for it.

[THE SYMBOLISM OF THE AREA]

And the shining one saith, 'Behold the explanation of the description of the area; we interpret each actual word spiritually and symbolically thus: The area of which he speaketh is CHRIST and MARY. CHRIST Himself is the vine, even as He said, 'I am the vine[1] of truth.' When He says 'thou shalt wash them with water', it hath reference to the baptism which is [in use] among us, and as concerneth that which he (MOSES) said, 'Thou shalt wash them with water when thou arrayest them in the vestments of the priesthood of the LEVITES.' When a man hath been baptized he can officiate as priest according to the Old [Law] and according to the New [Law]. When a man hath inhaled(?) [the Spirit[2]] thrice, he becometh like a babe which the impurity of sin hath never touched. And this saying is true, for the Apostles said, 'At midnight, [Fol. 23*a*, col. 1] when a man hath been baptized he becometh pure from his head to his feet. And when he hath not been baptized the Holy Ghost is grieved, and the angel who is associated (*or*, bound up) with him is also grieved.' And behold, this is an astounding saying.

[THE VESTMENTS OF AARON]

The holy vestments of AARON are to be interpreted as pure virgins. And the engraving on the seal must be interpreted as the seal on the Body of the Son, and the purple which is ornamented with flowers as the Incarnation of the Body of our Lord, even as SOLOMON saith, 'The grape-cluster which hath flowered of the son of my brother is mine', that is to say the flower of the Incarnation of our Lord.

---

[1] *'Aṣad* = area, court, field, and *'Aṣad wayen* = area of the vine, or vineyard; here there is a play on the words.

[2] A better reading is ʾ℞ⵏ: as the quotation from the Apostles shows.

The Place of Atonement

Now, the area towards the south is one hundred cubits [long], and surrounding it is an area towards the north twenty cubits [long] and the pillars [Fol. 23*a*, col. 2] and their bases were of brass. And towards the north-east is also an area twenty(?) cubits [long]. And the area which is towards the sea is seven(?) cubits [long], and the pillars and the areas which are towards the east are twenty cubits in width. The trumpets were of silver and the vestments of variegated stuffs.

[THE SYMBOLISM OF THE PILLARS, AND AREAS, AND TÂBÔT]

These pillars and these areas are to be interpreted as the Prophets and the Apostles. He saith, 'Pillars to the right of them and pillars to the left of them.' Those on the right are the Apostles, and those on the left are the Prophets, and those on the north-east are the Martyrs and those on the south the Priests. The TÂBÔT, which was closed with a bolt of gold, is MARY, who was sealed in chastity.

[THE PROPITIATORIUM]

And they shall make a place of atonement (*or*, propitiation) above the TÂBÔT (i.e. Ark or Tabernacle), and four CHERÛBÎM shall overshadow it [Fol. 23*b*, col. 1] [with their wings]. As the four CHERÛBHÎM overshadowed [with their wings] the place of atonement even so have the Four Evangelists ornamented the Church with the shadow of their teaching. As the Ten Words entered the TÂBÔT even so hath the Word of God dwelt in the womb of the Virgin.

[THE TABLE WITH FOUR GOLD RINGS]

The table which stood before it (i.e. the TÂBÔT) and was fastened thereto with ten (*sic*) rings of gold, [this] is the similitude of our Lord, the glorious Life, for the Scriptures call Him a table. ISAIAH saith,

Noah's Ark and the Tabernacle of Moses are related

'Lay out a table and eat ye.' And JOB saith, 'The table is fat' (i.e. provided with food in abundance). And DAVID saith, 'Thou hast prepared a table before me.' And the four (sic) gold rings of which he speaketh are the Four PÂPÂSÂT (Bishops?).

[THE LAMP OR CANDLESTICK]

And they shall make a standard for lamps, [Fol. 23b, col. 1] and branches on the right and on the left; and the standard, he saith, shall be of gold, and that is the Faith and the lamp on top of it is CHRIST. And the branches on the right and left of the standard symbolize the Law ('ÔRÎT) and the Prophets. And he saith, 'A twig shall go forth from its branches, three twigs'; the three branches are our Fathers the Apostles, the men of the Trinity.

[THE BRASS LAVER]

And they shall make a brass laver wherein [the people] shall wash their hands. Now the laver is the JORDAN, as SOLOMON saith, 'Thy navel is like a bowl which lacketh not drink', and by 'drink' he meant to say the Holy Ghost. And MÊRÊ'ÊBÊL is the name which is written on the Tabernacle, and this meaneth, 'Praised in name and praised in counsel.' The child of man who doth not wish for counsel is a fool.

[THE ARK OF NOAH AND THE SETTING UP OF THE TABERNACLE]

And God spake unto MOSES [Fol. 24a, col. 1] and said unto him: 'Thou shalt set up the Tabernacle at the beginning of the first month, for it was on the first day of the first month that NOAH established the Ark (TÂBÔT) and finished the building thereof. He finished it on . . .¹ the first month, and he and his family continued to go in until the sixteenth day. And on the seventeenth day

---

¹ The text is incomplete here, or perhaps the figures for two numerals have been omitted.

47

he shut the Ark. And having sent forth the raven it departed and did not come back. The angel told me the meaning of this passage and said unto me, The raven is SATAN who did not return to his habitation after he had gone forth [therefrom]. And the first dove is to be interpreted as the 'ôRÎT (Pentateuch), and the Prophets and their tabernacles. Then again, having been patient for seven days [NOAH] sent forth the dove; now the dove referred to here is the Holy Church. And the seven days which NOAH waited are the seven days [Fol. 24*a*, col. 2] from the second of the days of the Passion [of CHRIST] until His Resurrection.

[NOAH'S SACRIFICE]

And NOAH made a sacrifice, a young kid of the goats, and entreated God for the remission of the sin of all the world. Now the Ark of NOAH was not [made of] the wood of this world, but from a shoot of a tree which an eagle had cast [upon the earth].

[THE TÂBÔT OF MELCHISEDEK]

And the altar (TÂBÔT) of MELCHISEDEK was made of a block of sacred stone which the angels had consecrated and placed in the centre of the earth. Therefore did the Apostles say, 'Where the TÂBÔT of MELCHISEDEK is there will be the head of the Serpent.' The Serpent of which he speaketh is SATAN. And inasmuch as he saith it is there, he saith it because there did God cut in pieces the Serpent, even as PAUL saith, 'He killed the Enemy with His Cross.'

[THE RAM OFFERED UP BY NOAH]

The ram which was offered up instead of ISAAC was of [Fol. 24*b*, col. 1] the same kind (*or*, family) as the rams which ISRAEL sacrificed, and the ram which ABEL offered up. And that ram is a similitude of CHRIST; and these rams are rams of the Garden (Paradise).

The Tabernacle of Moses the Symbol of the Trinity

[MOSES SETS UP THE TABERNACLE]

And MOSES set up the *manbara* (i.e. place of abode) [formed of] curtains of gold. And he set the table, together with the equipment thereof, and the standard and its lights; and MOSES finished all his work. And the glory of God filled the cloud, and God sent His glory. And the cloud above it was the Holy Ghost; the equipment thereof was the Son, and its lights (candlestick)—its strengthener was the Father, the incense the prayer of the saints, and its anointing oil, the baptism, the Law of the Holy Church, that which belonged to Christians, which was made for them [Fol. 24*b*, col. 2]. And CHRIST was the completion of everything, and this is the whole of the work of the Tabernacle.

[THE OFFERINGS AT THE DEDICATION OF THE TABERNACLE]

And as concerning the dedication, they (i.e. the ISRAELITES) brought, each [tribe] according to their number, a bowl, of which the value was one hundred and thirty [shekels], and another of the value of seventy shekels, the shekels of the sanctuary, a vase of the value of ten shekels—now it was of gold and full of incense, and four rams, and five five [*sic*] oxen, and five rams, and five kids each [being] one year old, for an offering of salvation. These were their offerings which they brought.

[THE SYMBOLISM OF THE PRECEDING EXPLAINED]

And behold, the angel told me the explanation of the preceding. The twelve whom they brought for the dedication, on this side and on that in the Holy Church are the Twelve Apostles; they brought the whole world to their Lord. Instead of a bowl of silver there are in the New Law holy virgins. And [Fol. 25*a*, col. 1] instead of a bowl, a fountain of benefits, the remission [of sins] which is in the mouth of the priest. And instead of seventy shekels seventy disciples; and instead of an ox, CHRIST; and instead of a lamb, MARY; and instead of two rams, the learned teachers; and instead of the five cows, the five wise virgins; and instead of the five rams, the five loaves of bread; and instead of the two heifers, the two fishes which satisfied five thousand [people]; and instead of the five kids, the five alien nations who believed and were baptized; and instead of the sheep those women who have served our Lord with their possessions, whose names are, SALÔMÊ, and the MAGDALENE, and SÂRÂ, and YÔḤANNÂ, wife of KÔZÂ, and MÂRYÂM who anointed our Lord with scented unguent; and instead of MOSES, CHRIST [Fol. 25*a*, col. 2], and instead of AARON, PETER, the chief [of the Apostles], and instead of ÎYÂSÛ (JOSHUA), JOHN the Virgin.

[FURTHER EXPLANATION OF THE SYMBOLISM]

Now, it is impossible for one to describe every work of the Tabernacle, each in detail. And as PAUL saith, 'I have told thee very much, according as thou wast able to bear it.' And behold the following most excellent discourse:

Instead of a patera of gold, [there is] CHRIST; and the patera of gold, in value ten [shekels] of which he spoke, are the ten fingers of our Lord which He stretched out on the Cross; and in that he saith that it was full of incense, it showeth that our Lord prayed on the Cross and there and then destroyed the sins of the world. And the hands which MOSES raised up are to be interpreted as the hands of our Lord and AMALEK [Fol. 25*b*, col. 1]. And JOSHUA who went out to the war is to be interpreted as the Holy Ghost Who went forth to do battle with the evil ones. And AARON and ḤÔR who held up firmly the hands of MOSES are to be interpreted as the two thieves who were crucified with our Lord. Behold, this is the discourse which is for the men of understanding, and it is this which the Angel spoke to the blessed man BAKHAYLA MÎKÂ'ÊL. And the discourse on the Tabernacle and everything which relateth thereto is ended, and therein [will be found] wisdom, and understanding, and knowledge. The wise man who hath heard [it] will have added to [his] wisdom. [The Gospel] saith, 'He who hath an ear to hear, let him hear.' The first part describeth that which cometh last, and the last part completeth the first. One single word coming from one single homily. And in that it saith 'they made one seal', it showeth that the Gospel is [Fol. 25*b*, col. 2] the Seal of all the Scriptures.

Here I make an end for thee of the description of the mystery of the Tabernacle.

[EZEKIEL'S VISION OF THE TABERNACLE]

Now as concerning the Tabernacle the prophet hath seen a vision. EZEKIEL hath described the vision which he saw concerning JERU-SALEM. The people of JERUSALEM were divided into tribes according to the Twelve Peoples of ISRAEL. These represented the Twelve Apostles. The following are those who were [there]:

Twenty-five thousand head of the righteous at the first gate.

Ten thousand [at the second gate].

Twenty thousand at the third [gate].

Eighty-five thousand at the fourth [gate].

Twenty-five thousand at the fifth [gate].

Ten thousand [Fol. 26*a*, col. 1] at the sixth [gate].

Ten thousand at the seventh [gate].

Twenty-five thousand at the eighth [gate].

Forty thousand five hundred at the ninth [gate].

Forty thousand five hundred at the tenth [gate], [Fol. 26*a*, col. 1].

Four thousand and five at a tenth [gate] [*sic*].

Those who were in the neighbourhood of the area were four hundred, and there were five hundred in the west, and by the sea and those by the west were ten thousand, and those in the east did not pass over and did not remain in the area. And those who were in the south were ten thousand. And he telleth thee that in every gate there was a *têhê*, and by that *têhê* there were thirty on one side and thirty on the other, and he saith that by that *têhê* there were six on one side and six on the other, thirty on one side and thirty on the other. These are the sixty births of the Fathers (Patriarchs). When he saith *têhê* he meaneth effigy (*or*, portrait), and from *têhê* to *têhê* meaneth from effigy to effigy. The six on one side and the six on the other are the Twelve Apostles. And there are three companies who remain near the area who have righteousness in them, and they are the awarders of doom [Fol. 26*a*, col. 2]. And in the first [gate], and in all the [other] gates, those whose heads have been recorded, that is to say the righteous, and their angels, [their number is also recorded]. And from one *têhê* to another, there are some who draw near, and some who draw away according to their rank in righteousness; these are to be identified by the similarity of their thrones.

And he also said unto me, 'The righteous may not exceed seven ranks (*or*, grades), for every appointment of the priests is completed by the chief *pâpâs*, and the rank (*or*, grade) of the righteous is completed by [the number] seven. One gate is farther off than the other by one door (*or*, opening), and the measure (*or*, dignity?) of one righteous man is the double of that of this world, and of the gate through which the light cometh [Fol. 26*b*, col. 1]. And one giveth more light than the other. And some of the gates are of gold, and some of silver, and some of pearls, and some of crystal. Three of the gates are of gold and three of them are of silver. And one is higher than another, even as ISAIAH (chap. vi. 4) saith, 'The threshold of the door is raised up by the sound wherewith they cry out.' In all these gates the openings for egress are mixed (i.e. are different) and the souls of the righteous enter therein and come forth therefrom by the windows (i.e. openings) to JERUSALEM. And here are the channels wherefrom flow down into JERUSALEM, the honey, and the milk, and the wine, and the oil, and they run down into the Garden (i.e. Paradise) and water the whole earth.

And he (i.e. EZEKIEL) also saith unto thee: And to each limit (i.e. boundary) there was a *tôhî* and a vestibule, and six chambers facing the east and [six] facing [Fol. 26b, col. 2] the west, and two facing the north and two facing the south. The vestibule was five cubits, and the *'êpêmêdê*, and three gates. And the vestibule had twenty [cubits], and the breadth of the vestibule, the steps thereof, and the top of the vestibule each six [cubits]. The door of the *'êpêmêdê* five cubits, and its length one cubit(?), and the *'êpêmêdê* six [cubits] each way; the inside was six [cubits], each side was four [cubits]. And thirty-three steps equal [in height], and a party wall. And in front of the *'apôlîsu* was, as it were, a lake seventy cubits [in length] and five cubits broad. The *'apôlîsu* hath one hundred windows and openings with two or three CHERÛBHÎM by one *ṣabart*, which is palm-tree. And the wood of the altar had a height (*or*, length) of three cubits, and the length of the tables which were carved out of stone was one cubit and a half and their height was one cubit.

The explanation of the preceding is as follows: *'Êlâm* meaneth vestibule [Fol. 27a, col. 1]. By *'Êlâm* a chamber in four parts is meant. And the two *'êksedrê* are the two baskets of the offering (*or*, sacrifice) near the two CHERÛBHÎM. *'Êlâm* also meaneth a pillar, and *'êpêmêdê* signifieth a platform. *'Apôlîsu* is the sanctuary and *'îyâzkhâ*, a chamber.

[EXPLANATION OF THE SYMBOLISM]

The Spiritual interpretation is as follows: The two *'êksedrê* symbolize men, and describing them as two he meaneth the [two] natures of man. The *'êksedrê* which clothed man meaneth the right [hand] of the Father. And the *'êpêmêdê* is to be interpreted by the JORDAN; the three gates are the Trinity, and the *'êlâm* is to be inter-

53

preted by the Gospel. The twelve is to be interpreted the Twelve Apostles. When he speaketh of the finishing in six six (i.e. two sixes) he meaneth the six words which the saints use, and also the six words which the damned employ in their entreaties [Fol. 27*a*, col. 2]. And those who stand facing the right are the Christians who hold the right Faith; and those whom people call Christians but who do not hold the right Faith, their standing-place is facing the left. As for the wicked he doth not bring them into the argument because there is no retribution whereby they may be redeemed. And they come into SHEOL like running water, even as DAVID saith, 'Fire goeth in front of Him, and flame envelopeth His enemies.' And our Lord saith in the Gospel, 'Let the peoples (*or*, nations) be gathered together before Him.'

[THE DAY OF JUDGEMENT]

Concerning the Day of Judgement EZRA saith: 'From one side cometh joy, and from the other come judgement and punishment.' The names are five: SHEOL, darkness, punishment, which is an evil smoke, which is [Fol. 27*b*, col. 1] GAHÂNAM (GEHENNA); there remaineth the judgement which GAHÂNAM doth not swallow up. The judgement is the punishment of MUSLIMS and JEWS.

[THE VISION OF EZEKIEL—*continued*]

We will now return to our original matter. The seventy which he mentioneth for the *'êpêmêdês* are the Seventy Disciples. The four sides of which he speaketh are the four Evangelists who are equal in word (doctrine?). When he saith that the *'apôlîṣu* had seventy cubits he meaneth this world. For this reason EZEKIEL said, 'That day, after the Captivity, I saw a vision. And one took me up on a high mountain, whereon a city was built. And I came in and I found a man [there], and his face was like red-hot brass. And there was a measuring cord in [Fol. 27*b*, col. 2] one hand, and he had a measuring reed

54

in the other. And that reed stood up straight in the gateway, the height of which was six cubits, and the breadth thereof was likewise six cubits. He measured carefully the six steps with the reed, then the *têḥê*, then a second *têḥê*, and then a third *têḥê*, [comparing them] carefully with the first *têḥê*, then the *'êlâm* and the *'akhlî*, the completing portion of the gates. He looked at everything as far as he was able [to see].

The man whom he saw was the Son, and the reed which he saw is the word of the Gospel. The six cubits of which he speaketh are the six words whereby protection(?) cometh. The seven steps of which he speaketh are the seven ranks of the Church. When he saith that he stood in the gate, the gate is baptism. When he saith that its height [Fol. 28*a*, col. 1] and the breadth were equal, he meaneth that of all the words which God hath uttered, no matter on what subject, there is not one that is of less importance than the other in any particular. In saying that he measured carefully he showeth that everything hath been completed by the Gospel.

[THE ABODE OF THE ELECT WHO ARE SEALED]

As to the *têḥê* of which he speaketh, there the chosen ones are depicted, and those who are not there depicted are cast into the fire of GEHENNA. Every man who hath not the seal on his forehead—for him there is no hope of salvation. Every man who hath the seal on his forehead—the Son hath promised him that he shall be sealed.[1] For the Father said unto the Son, All those who are sealed with the blood of Thy side shall never be destroyed and shall never be made to suffer pain in SHEOL.

[DEATH]

Death is SATAN, even as PAUL saith, 'He hath fought that angel of Death, who is SATAN among the Christians' [Fol. 28*a*, col. 2]. This

---

[1] The text is corrupt here.

55

is a great mystery, surpassing everything. Those who have given alms, however small, for the sake of MARY, shall never perish.

[THE ORDINANCES AND THE BIRDS OF ISRAEL]

As concerning the ordinances of ISRAEL, hearken, I will tell thee. When AARON said, 'Let us praise Him', the birds of JUDAH made answer to his word, and they sang in a marvellous manner. The sweetness of their voices restored the heart and the people went up to hear them. And the birds of JUDAH which were in the camp with him amounted in number to one thousand doves, and three hundred birds of BÂBÎL, that is to say *'agôrgânât*, and two hundred turtle-doves.

And when AARON said, 'Hear, O heaven, and I will speak unto thee', the birds of REUBEN answered him, and their numbers were one thousand and three hundred birds of BÂBÎL, and the birds of JOSEPH were of like number [Fol. 28*b*, col. 1].

And again, when he said, 'The fire of my anger bursteth into flame' it was the birds of JOSEPH which answered his words.

And when AARON said, 'God shall bless thee', the birds of DÂN, NAPHTÂLÊM, and 'ASÊR answered his words. A marvellous work was wrought in the Tabernacle of ISRAEL. In days of old it was not all the birds which answered him at once, but only groups of ten, one ten after the other, but on days of high festival all the birds answered together. The food of the birds was provided by one tribe, each bird receiving ten *masparet*. The *masparet* is equal to the *ḥamôr* and according to the ETHIOPIANS and ABYSSINIANS the *masparet* is equal to two *'entalâm*. And one *îpha* also, one half [was given to them] in the morning, and the other half in the evening.

[THE KÔMÔN TREE]

The KÔMÔN tree was planted in the Tabernacle. And the priest went to it early each morning [Fol. 28*b*, col. 2] and said unto it, 'We

56

water thee with water', and that tree shot up with hope (i.e. con-
fidently); if the priest had not said these words the tree would not
have flourished. And when a man sacrificeth a sheep (*or*, lamb) as
a sin-offering, he roasts (*or*, boils) it with the wood of this tree; in
the case of other offerings another kind of wood is used.

[THE NINE MAGICAL NAMES]

This is the word which the angel of God said unto me: In order
that thou mayest not forget the word of God, and that thou mayest
have understanding, and that thy heart may uncover itself by the
word of God, and that thou mayest have knowledge, repeat the
following names:

'ADÂM	ZARÛDÂ'ÊL	BAZANADAKÂ'ÊL
NÂTNAW	DAPHLÂ	'AWLALÂ'ÊL
KABÎKÂ	ṬAṬÂ	'ÊLÂDÂ'ÊL

And having recited these names let him read DÂWÎT (i.e. DAVID, the
Psalter). He who shall bring a little water—let him drink and
swallow it without drawing breath. This have I told thee [Fol. 29*a*,
col. 1] and made thee to understand.

[THE TABERNACLE—*continued*]

Hearken [and] I will tell thee an astounding mystery concerning
the Tabernacle. The sacrifice was performed in the seventh area,
and as I have likewise related unto thee, where the *samâsaye*(?) is
and the altar(?) of the fire. The altar and the area may be described
as follows, and the ordinance relating to them.

The seventh tabernacle, that is KARÂ, hath nine pillars and
eighteen supports, and in it is an awesome furnace of the altar, and
its length (*or*, height) is. . . . Above it there is stretched out a sheet
of brass of equal length with eighteen openings in it; and below it is
a sheet of brass, and its length is ten hundred [cubits]. There also

I

are three cooking-pots, the first of gold, the second of silver, and the third of brass. And their sacrifices are performed in this Tabernacle of Testimony.

[EXPLANATION BY MOSES AND AARON]

The explanation of the preceding was told me by MOSES and AARON, and they said unto me: Hearken. When he saith to thee 'area' that meaneth the Holy Church [Fol. 29*a*, col. 2] as JOHN 'ABÛ ḲALAMSÎS (Apocalypse) saith, 'I have seen the churches.' And when he saith unto thee 'nine pillars' he referreth to the nine peoples who were carried off into captivity in the days of SELMENÂSÔR (SHALMANESER).

And the eighteen supports of which he speaketh mean:

1. Thou shalt not worship another.
2. Love.
3. Humility.
4. Gladness.
5. Graciousness.
6. Longsuffering.
7. Peace.
8. Faith.
9. Charitableness.
10. Suffering through excessive speech.
11. Fasting.
12. Steal not.
13. Be not proud.
14. Fornicate not.
15. Swear not false oaths.
16. What thou hatest do not to thy neighbour.
17. Honour thy father and mother.
18. Covet not all that thou seest.

[Fol. 29*b*, col. 1]. The man who keepeth all these commands shall inherit the kingdom of the heavens.

When he saith that there was an awesome furnace of the altar, the furnace is ADAM, and the fire is the God NÂR who dwelleth by his daughter. When he saith that its height was ten hundred [cubits] these [cubits] symbolize the ten hundred generations. When he saith a layer of brass is stretched out, the layer of brass is the Cross whereon our Saviour suffered. And he saith, 'He hath helped me on my bed of sickness.' And again he saith, 'He hath placed a bow of brass in my arms.' The twelve openings of which he speaketh are the twelve doors of heaven, even as the Prophets say. The four [*sic*] gates of heaven are DABRA ṢEYÔN, which yieldeth fruit ten times ten-thousand fold, and DABRA SÎNÂ, which yieldeth fruit ten times ten-thousand fold, and DABRA TÂBÔR, which yieldeth fruit forty times ten-thousand fold. And the bowl which is below it is instead of the Covenant [Fol. 29*b*, col. 2] or the belly of the believers.

As to the three cooking-pots of which he speaketh: the first one, which is of gold, representeth all the Apostles; the second, which is of silver, the Prophets; and the third, which is of brass, the Christians. When he saith that all the sacrifices were performed in the Tabernacle of Witness, he doth this to point out that the ordinances of the Church are fulfilled by the priests of every rank and grade; but it is not all of them who make offerings (*or*, perform sacrifices). The Apostle of this area is THADDEUS, the brother of JAMES, and the guardian of the altar is SALÂTYÂL.

[THE EIGHTH AREA]

The Eighth Area hath eight pillars and eight supports. In saying 'eight pillars' he meaneth the seven grades of the priesthood, and the eighth pillar is the Christian people. The eight supports of which he speaketh are the Seven Books of the Church, [Fol. 30*a*, col. 1] the Church itself being the eighth support.

[THE ORDINANCES OF THE LEVITES]

These are as follows: The high priest with forceps (*or*, a fork) bringeth the flesh out of the pot and casteth it down on the layer of brass. The fat drippeth down through the openings in it, and he maketh it run down and fill the three cooking-pots. And he maketh

59

to come three doves every Sabbath day, and he maketh them to inhale the odour of the altar. The first dove is red, the second is variegated in colour, and the third is white. And the high priest manifesteth wrath against the white dove, and he smiteth it, and killeth it, and saith unto it, 'She hath defiled my altar, and she hath destroyed all the threads (*or*, cords) of my tabernacle.'

[MOSES AND AARON EXPLAIN THE PRECEDING]

MOSES and AARON explained [this passage], and they said unto me: The Levites are the priests, and the high priest is the son of [Fol. 30*a*, col. 2] God, and the forceps (*or*, fork) is the word of the Gospel which seeketh after man as a believer. And the cooking-pot is the world, and the flesh is the peoples who cry out unto it (i.e. invoke it). And the fat which ran down is the Faith which is preached under the heavens. The three doves of which he speaketh are the three companies of the Prophets from ADAM to MOSES, from MOSES to [our] Lord, and from [our] Lord to the end of the world. The red dove of which he speaketh are the sacrifices of ISRAEL. Even as JOHN saith in his vision, 'There went forth a green horse, and the name of him who rode it was "Death", and SHEOL followed him.' Now the green horse which did not arrive at the area is the 'ÔRÎT (i.e. the Pentateuch of MOSES) [Fol. 30*b*, col. 1]. And the second dove which was variegated in colour (i.e. parti-coloured) is the Prophets and the sons of the Prophets, who have not found completely the baptism of life. For this reason the dove was not wholly white. And the third dove, which was white, is the Son of God who is innocent of sin. The priests who display wrath against it are the people who crucified Him, [viz.] the house of LEVI. When he saith that they said of the dove, 'It hath defiled my altar,' he meaneth the JEWS who say, 'It hath destroyed our Law and our doctrine.' And when they say, 'It hath destroyed every cord, the cord of my tabernacle,' it is indeed true that their 'ôrît hath been destroyed, and their prophecies, and their priesthood, and their kingdom, even as the Minister (*or*, Envoy) saith, 'Their 'ôrît is a worn-out thing, and their prophecies and their priests likewise.'

[THE LAW MADE NEW]

The Eternal Word of Life having risen from among the dead [Fol. 30*b*, col. 2] hath made new for us the ordinance (*or*, Law). We who believe have seen a marvellous thing, and moreover the priests on the day of their ordination see a hidden mystery. Some see Him in the form of a flame of fire, and some in the form of a babe, and some in the form of a bread cake [made of] the finest flour. The greater number of the priests see Him in the form of bread, and this is a marvellous mystery. And as concerning doves, there are two companies of prophets; they ascend out of SHEOL and they settle themselves to rest in the Tabernacle. Now this taketh place on Sabbath days. Similarly among Christians, there are some who have been (*or*, who are) sinners, and in whom there is a little of the grape; these shall not be repulsed.' [Those who have received] a little of the grape are those who have received the Faith [Fol. 31*a*, col. 1], that is to say the seal of baptism. Such shall not be destroyed.

[THE EIGHTH AREA *continued*]

ENOCH saith unto thee, 'The Sabbath which is righteousness' (*or*, justice, *or* truth). The meaning of this is, the Sabbaths of the Incarnation of the Son. When he saith 'a man cometh down into the area', he meaneth the Son. And this, 'In it he shall plant (*or*, set up) a straight mountain,' meaneth the Church, wherein is the true (*or*, orthodox) Faith. And the Apostle of this area is NATHANIEL, the son of CLEOPAS, and the angel thereof is a SERÂPHÎM, because on the eighth day in the eighth area, he had compassion on the SERÂPHÎM.

The Moabites

Here followeth the description of the Ninth Area, wherein are five columns and six supports. In this place standeth MÔ'AB the high priest, and here is planted the tree of [Fol. 31a, col. 2] KÔMÔN. The fruit thereof is as large as a horse-bean, and it is only fit to be used as an ingredient. Here too is the pomegranate, wherefrom goeth forth a juice which resembleth blood. When those who are possessed of an evil spirit drink therefrom they become cured of the disease of their sin. This juice hath perished and hath not been found since [the time of] MOSES.

MOSES and AARON explained this to me, and they said unto me: When he telleth thee of the ninth area it is the Church which is meant; in it there are seven grades of priests, and men and women who have believed. The five [sic] pillars of which he speaketh are PETER, JOHN, JACOB (JAMES), and JAMES the brother of our Lord. And the six supports are the six words of the Gospel which we employed in pleading a case(?) [Fol. 31b, col. 1]. When he speaketh to thee of MÔ'AB, he meaneth the Lord, the Father of everything, even as DAVID saith, 'MÔ'AB, the priest, is my hope [sic].' And again the MÔ'ABITES are to be interpreted as devils. Most certainly we do not assimulate them with the Lord, nay they betake themselves to flight whenever the Name of our Lord is mentioned. And 'MÔ'AB' meaneth 'fire', and the colour red is the symbol of the creation of the angels. And that the MÔ'ABITES are devils, hear the 'ÔRÎT, which saith, 'The angels whose name is MÔ'AB shall be blotted out.' And ISAIAH saith, 'In the night MÔ'AB shall be blotted out.' And the meaning of this is, when our Lord shall be crucified, the noonday shall become night. And then SHEOL shall be blotted out, and DIABOLUS shall be snared [Fol. 31b, col. 2] like a bird, and in the night they shall destroy the fortress of MÔ'AB.

Verily the Tabernacle hath been thrown down, and the fortress thereof, which is the 'ôrît, and even as hath been said, 'Remove its fortress.' And again ISAIAH saith, 'MOAB, be ye sorrowful for yourselves'; and verily the devils and those who crucified [our Lord] have sorrowed. And again ISAIAH, 'LADÊBÂN[1] hath been destroyed', that is to say, the synagogue hath been destroyed; [in it] was very much help which the 'ôrît and the Prophets had produced. The tree KÔMÔN, which he says was planted there, is the tree of prophecy. And when he saith that [the fruit] thereof was only useful as an ingredient he meaneth that the 'ôrît and the Prophets were of no use to ADAM and that they were unable to effect his salvation. The 'ôrît and the Prophets are called 'ingredient' because they were not actual food [Fol. 32a, col. 1]. CHRIST only is the Bread of Life, the Perfect Food. Because of this ISAIAH saith, 'They eat cumin with the wheat.' And verily, the prophecy of the Prophets hath been eaten up by the wheat of life, that is to say, CHRIST.

[THE TREE REMÂN]

When he saith, here is planted the tree REMÂN, he meaneth the tree 'ARYÂM (i.e. the Heaven-tree), and when he saith that when those who are possessed of devils have drunk [the juice] thereof they are healed, the meaning is that when the peoples have with faith drunk of His (i.e. CHRIST'S) blood they are healed of their sins. Now the devil who hath seized them and is their master is SATAN. And when he saith that that tree hath perished and hath not been found since the death of MOSES, he showeth that the water of life hath perished for those who crucified [CHRIST], but that it floweth continually for the believers [Fol. 32a, col. 2]. And it is because of this that the prophet said, 'The water of NÊMRÊM hath failed.' [Water of NÊMRÊM] meaneth 'water of mystery'. And again the prophet said, 'They have ascended the road of 'ARÔMÎN.' 'Verily the righteous

---

[1] Dibon(?) Isaiah xv. 2.

63

An Explanation by Moses and Aaron

have ascended the road of the heights' (i.e. heaven). And again ISAIAH saith, 'There shall be an earthquake', and in truth the Gospel saith that the earth quaked, and that many bodies of the righteous were raised up and came into the holy city upon the high road. The Apostle of this area is BARTHOLOMEW, the searcher into hidden things, and the angel is KHABERYÂNÔS, the great CHERÛB.

[THE TENTH AREA]

The following is [a description of] the Tenth Area. It hath four pillars, and is resplendent with brilliant light throughout. From it there extendeth a vapour (or, smoke) [Fol. 32b, col. 1] which is like unto a flame of fire. And this is what taketh place every year at the festival of the ear of corn. And the area hath six supports and six lamps. The meaning of this was described to me by MOSES and AARON, who said unto me: The four pillars of which he speaketh are the Holy Father and the light of the area is the Son, as the prophet saith, 'Send out thy light and thy justice (or, truth).' And again he saith, 'Thy right hand, thine arm, and the light of thy face.' And again he saith, 'Let light come from thy dwelling.' And the vapour (or, smoke), which is the similitude of the light, is the Holy Spirit, even as the Prophet saith. 'The vapour hath filled the house of his praise' (i.e. the house wherein he is praised). And JOHN [saith], 'The sanctuary is filled with praise and power.' And EZEKIEL saith, 'The altar was filled with smoke.' And PETER saith, 'Praise hath been sent with smoke.' And [Fol. 32b, col. 2] JEREMIAH saith, 'ADAM was shrouded in a vapour of smoke.' And again the prophet saith, 'From the north smoke shall go forth.' And what can the kings of the nations say except that they have defiled it? And when he saith, 'the festival of the ear of corn' he meaneth that likewise in the New Law, at the festival of Pentecost the Holy Spirit descendeth at the time of the third hour, at the time of the raising up of the Offering.

Further Explanation by Moses and Aaron

The three supports of which he speaketh are the three heavens, even as the maintainers of the world say, 'We have taken clean water, and have created three heavens therewith, and [we have created] other heavens with a flame of fire'.

The seven lamps of which he speaketh are the seven tabernacles of fire, the curtains [which] hide the Trinity. And this [Tenth] Area is the station (i.e. permanent basis) of the righteous and of the children of ḲÂ'ÂT. And ḲÂ'ÂT begot LÊWÎ. And 'ENBARÂM begot MOSES and [Fol. 33a, col. 1] AARON and MÂRYÂM (MIRIAM). And MOSES begot GÊRSAM and 'ÊLYAZÂR. And AARON begot NÂDÂB and 'ABDEYÂ. And 'AL'ÂZÂR begot PHÎNÂḤAS. And PHÎNÂḤAS begot 'ABSÊ. And 'ABSÊ begot BÂḲÂ. And BÂḲÂ [begot] ṬÂMREN. And ṬÂMREN begot 'AḲÎ-MÊLÊK. And there were priests, sons of the Law, and the Ordinance; and [the names of] these and others likewise are written in the Book of Chronicles. And the Apostle of this area is PHILIP, [a name meaning 'man of understanding' and 'young man']; and the angel is SADÂḲÎYÂL, the comforter of those suffering tribulation.

Here is [a description of] the Eleventh Area: It hath eight pillars and forty-nine supports. MOSES and AARON described the meaning thereof, and they told me: The five of the eight pillars of which he speaketh are the 'ÔRÎT of MOSES. Of the three remaining pillars, the first is the [Book of] JOSHUA [Fol. 33a, col. 2], the second is the [Book of the] JUDGES, and the third is the [Book of] RUTH. The forty-nine supports of which he speaketh are the forty-nine Books of the Prophets. Now this number of forty-nine is made up by [the Books of] the Eight Prophets who knew what had taken place in the past, and what would take place in the future. And one of them said, 'The king of the south shall go to the king of the north. And she shall contract marriage with him. And the two kings shall converse together with falsehood at a feast, and because of this a mighty slaughter shall take place between them.' MOSES and AARON told me the meaning of this [prophecy] and they said unto me: The king of the south is a RÔMÂWÎ who dwelleth towards the south of heaven and to the west of the same. And now he is his vassal, and they have acted wickedly towards him for six years and five. An envoy (*or*, ambassador) shall come [bearing] a liar-name (i.e. false name). And two [years] after he hath come, the king of the south [shall come bearing] a liar-name, and he shall be of the issue of JAPHET, [Fol. 33*b*, col. 1] as EZEKIEL saith, '. . . shall go forth from JAPHET'. When he saith, 'The two of them shall talk falsehood at one table', he meaneth that the king of the south shall say to him, 'When I have seized the king of ETHIOPIA I will give him unto thee.' And the king of the north shall say unto him, 'I will give thee seven thousand horses.' They have tricked each other, and therefore a great slaughter shall take place between them. And that woman shall take to flight on a horse and return to her father. And the king of the south shall break his friendship with the king of ETHIOPIA, for they shall have in their hands the spear and the cross. And when he seeth this sign the man with the false name shall flee from them, and then he will gather together the wrath of all the nations. And then will come the Lord and His army with Him, and they will fight [Fol. 33*b*, col. 2] with him, and will drive away the man with a false name from his kingdom. And they will wipe out his soldiers and he himself shall be cast into the fire, even as the Apostles say. And after this there shall be a new heaven and a new earth. And this [Eleventh Area] shall be the fixed abode of the children of ISSACHAR. And He shall destroy the son of ḲÂʿÂT, and [*sic*] ḲÂʿÂT, the son of LÊWÎ; and He shall destroy the son of FÂḲÛRÂ and ḲÔRÊ, and ḲÔRÊ the son of FÂRÊG, and FÂRÊG TÂMMÛZ, and TÂMMÛZ FÊLÊTO. And these have been burnt in the fire, and there are left none except the children of NÂMÛÊL. And NÂMÛÊL begot 'ÊLFÂSÂFÎ, and he is the father of many.

The Twelfth Area hath four columns and twelve supports. Here followeth the explanation of the same: The four pillars of [Fol. 34*a*, col. 1] which he speaketh are chief PÂPÂSÂT. Instead of the Four Beasts there are four thrones. Instead of the Four Rivers, the four meadows of the Gospel. Instead of the Four Winds of heaven, the four corners (angles) of the earth. Instead of the Four Chariots of the CHERÛBHÎM, the four angles of the Cross. Instead of the Four Balancers of the sun, the four angles of the TÂBÔT. Instead of the Four Rivers of fire, the four angles of the Church. Instead of the Four Pillars of the moon, the four stones which were on the vestment of AARON. Instead of the Four Camps of heaven, the four camps (*or*, companies) of ISRAEL when they were on the march [from EGYPT]. [Instead of] the Four Trumpets, the four pangs of pain of the hands and feet of our Lord. Instead of the Four Gates of heaven, the four faces of heaven [Fol. 34*a*, col. 2]. Instead of the Four Trees of the Garden (Paradise), the four ḲASFÂ which are given on the day of baptism, the milk, the honey, the flesh, and the blood. Instead of the Four Windows of glass, the hundred candles of the Church. Instead of the Four Angels who stand on the four sides of the Lord of spirits, the four elements (*or*, natural substances) of the creation of the world, and those who were created from each of them. Glory and praise be to the Handicraftsman who created this [universe]! And everything subsists through the Trinity.

The Twelve Supports of which he speaketh are the Twelve Apostles. The Area is the fixed abode of 'AZÂḤÊL, the son of ḲÂ'ÂT, the son of LÊWÎ. And 'AZÂḤÊL was the son of NÊS, being born in the month of NÊSÂN. And NÊSÂN begot 'AYÂB, and 'AYÂB begot PÂKÔN, and PÂKÔN begot DABR, and DABR [Fol. 34*b*, col. 1] begot NÂR, and

An Explanation by Moses and Aaron

NÂR begot WÊLES. And the Apostle of this Area is JAMES, the son of ALPHAEUS, and the angel thereof is 'AḴÂMYÂL, the Keeper of the Garden (Paradise).

[THE THIRTEENTH AREA]

Here followeth a description of the Thirteenth Area which hath three hundred and eighteen supports. The colour thereof is white, like the flower of the rose, and one of the supports at certain times appeareth in the middle of them.

[THE EXPLANATION BY MOSES AND AARON]

MOSES and AARON related to me this explanation, and they said unto me: The pillars of which he speaketh are the 'ÔRÎT, the Prophets, and the Apostles, and the three hundred and eighteen supports mentioned are the Three Hundred and Eighteen orthodox Fathers [of the Council of NICAEA]. When he saith that their colour is white like the flower of the rose, it is because the flower of the rose is white, and the teaching of the Three Hundred and Eighteen Fathers is like [the light of] the sun, and when he saith that one support sometimes appeareth among them and [Fol. 34b, col. 2] and sometimes doth not appear, his allusion is to our Lord and our God. Sometimes He appeareth among them, and sometimes He hideth Himself from them, and sometimes they are three hundred and eighteen [in number]. And it happeneth in this wise so that they may know that He is the Lord. This Area is the fixed abode of the children of KÊBRÔN, the son of 'ÂRÊN, and ['ÂRÔN] of 'AMḤAN and 'AMḤAN of TEGRÂN, and 'ALHÎZ and SÊWÊN, the son of WÂKER. And the Apostle [of this Area] is PAUL, and 'AKYÂL is the angel thereof.

[THE FOURTEENTH AREA]

Here followeth a description of the Fourteenth Area wherein are

68

two pillars, one large and the other small, which are like the rind of a pomegranate, and it hath three supports.

[THE EXPLANATION BY MOSES AND AARON]

MOSES and AARON related unto me the explanation, and they said unto me: The two pillars of which he speaketh are the two companies of the martyrs [Fol. 35a, col. 1], those of ANTIOCH and those in JERUSALEM. The large pillar of which he speaketh is the martyrs of ANTIOCH, and the small pillar of which he speaketh are the babe martyrs of JERUSALEM. The colour of the pillars spoken of by him, viz. [that of] the rind of the pomegranate, is the symbol of the shedding of the blood of the martyrs. And the three supports of which he speaketh are the symbol of the Trinity whom the martyrs guard. But the martyrs of ANTIOCH are greater than the martyrs of JERUSALEM, both in our estimation and in that of the Most High Himself, who knoweth which are the greater. And very many of the children who became martyrs kept their virginity, and men speak more especially of THEODORE who never lay with [Fol. 35a, col. 2] a woman, and never ejected seed on a woman except during a dream of the night. Or when his companions preceded him while he was teaching himself the Book (i.e. the Scriptures); when weeping he saw the gift of heaven. The following names are [written] in the Tabernacle: they say (i.e. read) ṢABÂ'ÔT (SABAOTH) and SADDÂY, and one saith SAMUEL.

[THE FIFTEENTH AREA]

Here followeth a description of the Fifteenth Area. It hath two pillars, one having a colour resembling that of water, and the other blazeth like fire. The two pillars have one support.

[THE EXPLANATION BY MOSES AND AARON]

MOSES and AARON described to me this explanation, and they said

The Effigies of the Saints in Heaven

unto me: The two pillars of which he speaketh are ELIJAH and JOHN, and the pillar which blazed like fire is ELIJAH whose heart was set on fire because of his jealousy for God. When he saith that one [Fol. 35*b*, col. 1] pillar was of the colour of water he meaneth JOHN, who baptized the people with water. And when he saith that the support of the two pillars was one he meaneth the leather girdle which each of them wore. This Area belongeth to the children of MÎRÂRÎ. And MÎRÂRÎ begot KHÂMÛSÎ, and LÔBÎNÎ begot SEMEY. According to what one saith, the 'tabernacle of MÂ'ÊL' meaneth 'Hearer of prayers'.

[THE SIXTEENTH AREA]

Here followeth a description of the Sixteenth Area. In it there are four pillars and five hundred doves, of which four hundred are white and one hundred black, and two supports.

[THE EXPLANATION BY MOSES AND AARON]

MOSES and AARON described to me this explanation. The four Teachers of whom he speaketh are MACARIUS, ANTHONY, SÎNÔDÂ (SHENÛTÎ), and PACHOMIUS. The four hundred white doves are the children of these four Teachers, and the one hundred black doves are the monks [Fol. 35*b*, col. 2] who came after [them]. The two supports are fastings and prayer of the saints. And inside it (i.e. the Area) are painted the effigies of the saints. First [cometh]

'ADÂM	SÊT	HÊNÔK [*sic*]	ḲÂYNÂN
MALAL'ÊL	YÂRÊD	HÊNÔK	'MÂTÛSÂLÂ
LÂMÊKH	NÔKLA	SÊM	'ALPHÂKSAD
ḲÂYNÂM	SÂLÂ	'ĔBÊR	PHÂLÊK
RÂGW	SÊRÔKH	NÂKÔR	TÂRÂ
'ABRĔHÂM	YESḤAḲ	YÂ'ĂḲÔB	

These drew lots and they painted inside the Tabernacle [the man to whom] the lot came.

The Effigies of the Saints in Heaven

And as concerneth the Fathers (Patriarchs) the Angel of the Face painted them—and after:

YEHÛDÂ	PHÂRÊS	'ÊSRÔM	'ARÂM
AMÎNÂDÂB	'ASÔN	SALÔMÔN	BA'ÊZ
'ÎYABÊD	'ĔSÊY	DÂWÎT	SALÔMÔN
RÔB'AM	'ABEYÂ	'ASAPH	'ÎYÔSÂPHAṬ
'ÎYÔRÂM	'ÎYABÊD	[Fol. 36a, col. 1]	'AMÊS
'AZARYÂS	'ÂZAYÂN	'ÔZYÂN	'ÎYÔ'TÂM
'AKÂZ	ḤEZḴEYÂS	MENÂSÊ	'AMÔṢ
'ÎYÔSYÂS	'ÎKÔNYÂN	SALÂTYÂL	ZARÛBÂBÊL
'ABYÛD	'ÊLYÔḴÊM	'AZAR	SADÔḴ
'ÂL'ÂZAR	'ÊLYÛD	'AKÎM	'AL'ÂZAR
MÂTÂN	YÂ'AḴÔB and YÔSÊPH.		

And these are written in the Gospel (Luke iii. 34–8); they were saved because [they were of] the kin of MARY, the Virgin.

[THE SEVENTEENTH AREA]

Thus did they describe it to me. There are in it three pillars, and the first pillar hath eight supports, and the second column two, and the third column twelve.

[THE EXPLANATION]

The explanation is as follows: When he saith 'three pillars' they are ABRAHAM, ISAAC, and JACOB; and when he saith that the first pillar hath eight supports, these are [Fol. 36a, col. 2] the children of ABRAHAM—six by KÊṬÛRÂ, one by SARÂ, and one by 'AGÂR. Now their names were: ZANBAR, YÂKENS, MÂDAY, and MÂDÂN, 'ÎYAZEBAḴ, SÊḤYÂ, YESMÂ'ÊL, and YESḤAḴ. When he saith that the second pillar has two supports, these are the children of ISAAC, i.e. JACOB and ESAU. And when he saith that the third pillar hath twelve supports, these are the children of JACOB.

71

Stones symbolizing the Patriarchs

These are all the mysteries of the Tabernacle such as the Angel of God hath described them unto me.

[THE SETTLEMENTS OF THE TWELVE TRIBES]

And the people established themselves, each tribe in its own place. The tribe of JUDAH, and those who encamped with them, established themselves towards the East.

And the tribe of REUBEN, and those who encamped with them, [Fol. 36b, col. 1] each tribe by itself, established themselves on the right hand.

And the tribe of JOSEPH, and those who encamped with them, established themselves towards the sea (i.e. the west).

And the tribe of DAN, and those who encamped with them, established themselves in the region behind, to the west of the Tabernacle. The order which they observed when on the march they kept when they halted, and they did not invade the Seventh Area where the altar was.

And these Patriarchs were depicted (or, symbolized) on the vestment of AARON:

JUDAH by a sardion.

ISSACHAR by a topaz.

ZEBULON by an emerald.

'ATÂ and REUBEN by a jasper.

SIMEON and LEVI by a coal-like stone.

GAD by a sapphire [set separately?]

JOSEPH by an amethyst.

ZEBULON by an agate(?)

MENASSEH by a ṭelem.

GAD [sic] by an 'aḳtâ bêta mênês.

NAPHTALI by an onyx.

And ASHER by a beryl [Fol. 36b, col. 2].

72

Meanings of the Names of Patriarchal Stones

The significations of these stones are as follows:

The sardion—his foundation hath been laid by God.

The topaz—relates the sufferings (i.e. the Passion) of the Only One.

The emerald—testeth(?) with fire.

The jasper—it hath sworn with words over many.

The stone like coal—the zeal of the priests.

The sapphire—we worship in the place where the foot of our Lord hath stood.

The amethyst—the ear of wheat hath flowered before its season.

Agate—it hath crushed the believers, and afterwards it hath itself believed.

Ṭelem—it hath acted craftily(?) like a hook among a number of others like unto it.

'Aḵtemâ—[Fol. 37a, col. 1] it hath killed God.

Tebê—make manifest to us His handicraft.

These are the significations (or, symbolisms) [of these stones], and this is a marvellous mystery.

And the Apostle of this Area is STEPHEN, and the angel thereof is he who hath held converse with me.

[THE THREE PILLARS AND THEIR NAMES]

The first pillar of which he speaketh is BERSEBÂḤÊ PÎLELÔS; the second pillar is called 'ÊSÊDÊRÊS, and chief of the priests of ISRAEL; and the third pillar is called WANÂṬÎ'Ê-'A'Ḵ-ḤABATÊR. Here are the explanations of these names:

BERSEBÂḤÊ meaneth, 'The Father Who is praised by the Son.'

PÎLÔS (PÎLELÔS) meaneth, 'Their praises [come] from them.'

'ÊSÊDÎRÔS [sic] meaneth, 'The Father doth not precede the Son', and 'the right of the Father [is] the Son', and when he saith that He is the first of the chiefs [Fol. 37a, col. 2] of ISRAEL, he meaneth that it is He who rose up among the Apostles, even though the doors were shut. Even as DAVID saith, 'God hath stood up in the assembly of the gods.'

TÎNÔṬÎKÎ meaneth the 'balsam which the Holy Spirit hath been for us'.

'AKLABÊPÊR meaneth, 'the sanctifier of body and soul'.

[THE SIGN OF THE CROSS AND THE TRINITY]

I make the Sign of the Cross over myself, and I declare openly [my belief in] the Trinity. And I believe in this Trinity which consisteth of Three Persons and One Godhead, and one kingdom, and one power, and one lordship, and one will, and one wish, three phases and one single aspect, and three beings and one name, one in equality and one in their wholeness, even as one saith, 'The sun dwelleth in the heavens and the light thereof dwelleth on the earth, and [Fol. 37b, col. 1] the fire thereof maketh hot.' By this similitude the Trinity may be known.

[THE 'ÔRÎT OF MOSES]

There are four supports in the TÂBÔT wherein is the 'ÔRÎT. The chest of gold [containing] the manna; the rod of AARON which blossomed; the censer of gold; and the whip with four cords. [These are] symbols (*or*, pictures) of the Four CHERÛBHÎM and a mountain of the colour of white crystal above the TÂBÔT.

[THE EXPLANATION OF THE PRECEDING]

Behold the explanation thereof: The four supports of which he speaketh are the four Books which EZRA wrote when he saith the TÂBÔT, that is the New Ark, the chaste MÂRYÂM. There is the TÂBÔT of MOSES, and here are we, the Ark of the Holy Spirit, even as PAUL saith, 'We are the *tâbôt* of the Holy Spirit, the CHRIST.' There only the Ten Words (i.e. Ten Commandments) were [to be found] in the belly of the TÂBÔT, but here [Fol. 37b, col. 2] is the Word of the Father; the One and Only Son in the womb of MARY. Even as the Book of Kings saith (1 Kings viii. 9), 'There was nothing inside the Ark except the Ten Words.' The omer is symbolic of the Church; the manna therein is the Body of the Son; the cover of gold thereof is the Apostles; the staff of AARON which blossomed is to be interpreted as the key of PETER; and the rod of MOSES by the Cross of CHRIST. The rod of MOSES which smote the sea made ISRAEL to pass over, and the Cross of CHRIST which smote the head of the serpent, that is to say SATAN, made the nations to pass over from death into life. There the rod of MOSES wrought ten miracles, and here [Fol. 38a, col. 1] the Cross of CHRIST smashed the heads of ten devils.

The whip of cords of which he speaketh showeth that there they punished the man who had transgressed with forty stripes, even as saith the 'ÔRÎT, 'If any man hath shown irreverence to the [oil of] MÊRÔN they shall scourge him with one hundred and forty and three stripes. And if a man hath drunk thereof in order [to effect] a healing, they shall take him to [a place whence] he cannot return, and bring him where they can kill him.'

[THE FOUR CHERÛBHÎM]

The Four CHERÛBHÎM are the Four Evangelists. When he speaketh of the mountain of white crystal which was upon the mountain, the mountain meaneth a cloud. And when he saith that it was of the colour of crystal, he meaneth the children of baptism. When [JOHN] baptized our Redeemer, a bright cloud overshadowed His head, even as the Evangelist saith, 'A bright cloud came and overshadowed them' [Fol. 38a, col. 2] (Matthew xvii. 5). And Paul saith, 'And we also have witnesses who surround us like a cloud' (Hebrews xii. 1). And the 'ÔRÎT saith, 'The Tabernacle was covered by a cloud' (Exodus xl. 32). And JOB saith, 'An exceedingly bright cloud [all at] once'. And ZACHARIAH saith, 'He hath raised up from the cloud His saints.' And DAVID saith, 'He guided them in the daytime by a cloud' (Psalm cxxvii. 14). And SOLOMON saith, 'The cloud hath let drop the dew' (Proverbs iii. 20). And ISAIAH saith, 'I will overshadow my people with a cloud' (iv. 5, 6).

[THE BELOVED VINE OF ISRAEL]

And again ISAIAH saith, 'The beloved one had a vineyard in a rich country. I girded it about with a girdle made of hard stones, and surrounded it with a fence, and I planted therein a chosen vine which was of the finest growth(?), and I built a tower in the middle of the vineyard. Then I waited for it to bring forth clusters of grapes [Fol. 38*b*, col. 1], and it hath yielded thorns. Judge between Me and My vineyard saith God' (Isaiah v. 1, 2).

Here is the explanation: The vineyard of which he speaketh is ISRAEL, even as this prophet saith, and the rich country is JERUSALEM wherefrom the dew of life from the heights of heaven hath descended. When he saith, I have girded it about with a girdle of hard stones, he meaneth that ISRAEL made in the desert a layer of brass the length of which was seventy cubits, and piled dust upon it. And there they planted a vine as DAVID saith, 'They have planted a vine and sown the fields with seed' (Psalm cvi. 27). And when the days were ended they watered it with water, and when they set out on the march He marched with them, and raised Himself by the command of God, the Holy Ghost. And this ordinance [Fol. 38*b*, col. 2] continued until the death of MOSES.

[THE FESTIVALS OF ISRAEL]

The whole social state of ISRAEL was governed by ordinances. Their festivals were the Passover, unleavened bread, the festival of the ear of wheat, the blowing of trumpets, the festival of Bader, the festival of tabernacles, and the Sabbath (Leviticus, chap. xx). At every festival all the people gather together, and swear oaths in the Tabernacle. And on that day the high priest taketh a red heifer whereon yoke hath never been laid (Numbers, chap. xix) and he saith, 'This beast is a ransom for the sins of all the people', and he slaughtereth it, [he being held to be] unclean. And those who held it were unclean, and he who touched it was unclean, and he who sacrificed it was unclean, and he who poured out the blood was unclean, and he who sprinkled the people with the blood was unclean, but the people who [Fol. 39a, col. 1] were sprinkled with the blood were holy, a matter whereat to wonder.

[THE EXPLANATION OF THE PRECEDING]

Behold the explanation: The red heifer of which he speaketh is MARY. When he saith that it hath not suffered a yoke to be laid upon it, this meaneth that MARY had never known a man. And as MARY is symbolized by the red heifer, so likewise our Lord is also so symbolized because He put on the flesh of MARY. And those who sacrificed [the heifer] are the crucifiers [of our Lord], that is the confederacy (*or*, synagogue) of the JEWS. And the people who are sprinkled with the blood are the people of the Christians, who are the Saints.

And on that same day the high priest would go into the Holy of Holies. And there would go in with him a priest whom he had chosen, and a chosen virgin [Fol. 39a, col. 2]. And in the hands of the virgin they placed a branch of a vine and an ear of wheat. And [having put on] the head-cloth he said, 'Let a sign be given'; [such was] his word to the people.

[EXPLANATION OF THE PRECEDING]

The explanation is as follows: The high priest is CHRIST. The Holy of Holies is holy baptism. The priest who is on the right hand

The Virgin Mary, the Vine Branch, and the Wheat Ear

is the symbol of JOHN the Baptist. The chosen virgin is the symbol of the priest MELCHISEDEK. The vine branch and the ear of wheat are the symbols of bread and wine. And when MELCHISEDEK spake and said to the people, 'Let a sign be given', he meant the sign of His (i.e. CHRIST's) Body and Blood which MELCHISEDEK gave to ABRAHAM. And [Fol. 39b, col. 1] it is in reference to this that DAVID saith, 'Thou art his priest for ever, according to the appointment of MELCHISEDEK' (Psalm cix. 4).

And ISAIAH saith, 'He shall come to the city of ḤAGÊ, he shall pass on to MAGÊDÔN, he shall make to remain his possessions in MEKMÂS, and shall pass on into the lowlands. He shall appear as from the mountains (*or*, seen in the mountains), he shall raise himself up above the hills, and on his arrival at ḤAGÊ, RÊMÂ, the city of SAMUEL, shall be afraid. The daughter of GÂLÂN shall take to flight, and one shall hear [of her] in 'ÊSÔN and 'ANÂTÔT, and the MANDÊNÂWÎ-YÂN shall quake with fear (see Isaiah x. 28 ff.).

[EXPLANATION OF THE PRECEDING]

The explanation is as follows: ḤAGÊ is the angel of life. The city is the world. MAGÊDÔN is the umbilicus of the earth. When he saith that he shall make his possessions to remain in MEKMÂS, he meaneth the possessions of the Son [Fol. 39b, col. 2] which are the Body of the Son and His Blood, which He hath shown having made them to remain with MELCHISEDEK. The lowlands are the people, and with reference to this DAVID saith, 'The lowlands (i.e. the valleys) are full of wheat' (Psalm lxiv. 14). The wheat is the word of God. The mountains are the Prophets and the hills are the Apostles. When he saith that on his arrival at ḤAGÊ, RÊMÂ, the city of SAMUEL, shall be afraid, he meaneth that at the arrival of our Lord in SHEOL the tribes of SEṬNÂ'ÊL, who have descended from RÊMÂ, were terrified. And SAMUEL [symbolizes] ADAM. 'The daughter of GÂLÂN who fleeth' is

SHEOL. GÂLÂN means a young man, and young man means sin, that is SATAN [Fol. 40a, col. 1]. JOB saith that SATAN was a young man: 'and he standeth up like a vigorous young man'. SOLOMON also saith, 'Woe be unto thee, O city, [when] thy king is a young man' (Ecclesiastes x. 1). And 'one shall hear of him in 'ÊNSÔN and 'ANÂTÔT', the meaning is that the coming of the Son was known in the 'ÔRÎT. And the MANDÊNÂWÎYÂN who shall quake with fear are the devils and the crucifiers [of CHRIST] who were terrified when they knew that the Son had risen.

[THE RESURRECTION]

With reference to the Resurrection ISAIAH saith, 'Now will I arise, saith God, Now I am glorious, now I am exalted on high, and now ye shall see, and now ye shall know' (Isaiah xxxiii. 10). And with reference to His Passion ISAIAH saith, 'He hath come like a lamb which is to be slaughtered, and like a sheep which hath not bleated before him that will shear him, he hath not [Fol. 40a, col. 2] opened his mouth in his suffering' (Isaiah liii. 7). And again ISAIAH saith with reference to the Passion of the Son, 'O ye wealthy women, rise up and hear ye my voice. O ye believing maidens, give ye attention to my discourse' (Isaiah xxxii. 9). 'And at each festival each year, make a commemoration of me, taking care [to think] of the day of my passion.'

[THE EXPLANATION]

And the explanation which they told me is as follows: When he saith 'wealthy women', these are the Christian Churches which are rich through the Two Laws, the Old and the New, as well as through the glory of God. When he saith, 'Hear ye my voice', the voice is that of the Gospel. When he saith 'maidens' these are the souls of the righteous (*or*, justified). When he saith 'make a commemoration of me each year' that is the Passover, the commemoration of His Resurrection. When he saith, 'Taking care to think of the day of my Passion', [Fol. 40*b*, col. 1] this hath reference to what our Lord said, 'Tell the story of my death until I come [again'].

And ISAIAH saith unto thee openly, 'Seven women shall lay hold upon one man, [saying], We will eat our own bread, and we will array ourselves in our own garments, only let us be called by thy name, and make us to put aside the disgrace [of virginity?]' (Isaiah iv. 1). In that day they shall shine in the counsel of his glory (*or*, praise).

[THE EXPLANATION]

Behold the explanation. The seven women of whom he speaketh are the seven grades of the Church. The 'food' is the word of God. As PAUL saith, 'There are they who were baptized in CHRIST; ye have clothed yourselves with CHRIST.' When he saith, 'Make us to put aside disgrace', that is, let us not fight with rams and bulls. The light [with which they shall shine] is the Apostles, even as He Himself said unto them [Fol. 40*b*, col. 2], 'Ye are the light of the world' (Matthew v. 14). The 'remainder of SION' are the Christians who remain, that is who are saved.

[THE EAGLE AT LEBANON]

And ISAIAH saith unto thee openly, 'Make ye to grow out wings like the eagle' (Isaiah xl. 31). And as concerneth the eagle EZEKIEL saith, 'This great eagle with the great wings and full-[grown] claws hath come into LIBANUS and carried off the choice part of the cedar, and hath cut it in its midst, where the tender [shoots] are' (Ezekiel xvii. 3).

[THE EXPLANATION]

And behold [the explanation]: The eagle is the spirit, and his wings are the Prophets, and his claws are the Apostles. In former times (*or*, of old) at [the festival] of BADER of ISRAEL he flew about for two hours, and he departed having slit the veil (*or*, curtain). But from the time when they crucified our Lord he hath not returned to them, even as saith the prophet, 'The spirit since it hath gone forth will not return.' And the Prophets [Fol. 41*a*, col. 1] also have prophesied concerning the coming of the Son. And MOSES said, 'Ye shall see him with your own eyes. He who hath not seen the sign of the serpent shall die, and he who hath seen it shall not die.' The Evangelist saith, 'He who hath seen the Son and hath believed on Him shall live for ever. And he who hath not believed on Him, and hath not seen Him shall die' (John vi. 40). The Evangelist saith unto thee openly, 'As MOSES hung up the serpent in the desert, even so the son of man shall be hung up' (John iii. 14).

And ISAIAH saith, 'He came, he was slaughtered like a lamb', and these words have reference to the hanging up [on the Cross] of our Lord. And JEREMIAH said, 'I am like a simple sheep, and they take evil counsel together against me, and say, We will put wood into his bread' (Jeremiah xi. 19). The wood is the Cross, and the bread is CHRIST even as He Himself saith, 'I am the bread of life [Fol. 41*a*, col. 2] which came down from heaven' (John vi. 51). The jealous one and avenger shall take vengeance on behalf of ABEL. God saith, 'Whosoever shall avenge CAIN sevenfold, LAMECH shall be avenged seventy-seven times' (Genesis iv. 24).

[THE EXPLANATION]

And behold the explanation: LAMECH was a blind man and is the symbol of SATAN, and likewise CAIN was the symbol of ADAM his father. LAMECH killed CAIN, SATAN killed ADAM by the eating of [the fruit of] the tree. In the days of LAMECH came the water flood, [through] seven cataracts from heaven and seven from the earth. And as LAMECH [suffered] seven times more than ADAM, so SATAN

St. Peter explains the Incarnation

[shall suffer] seven times more than the act which was wrought on the first day [of the week, i.e. Sunday]. And for the avenging of LAMECH, as it were, CHRIST, the offspring of the Patriarchs, hath come, mounted upon seventy and seven pearls, to take vengeance on SATAN. And the seventy and seven pearls are those which LUKE, the Evangelist, mentions [Fol. 41b, col. 1]. And the two wives must be interpreted by the people of KÂM and JAPHET. And the man whom he killed is ADAM, and the young man is ABEL. 'He who hath understanding let him understand'—saith ABBÂ BAṢALÔTA MÎKÂ'ÊL.

[EXPLANATION OF THE INCARNATION]

And some time after this PETER was sent unto me, and he said unto me:—'I am going to make thee to understand how the Only One took upon Himself flesh. The Father, and the Son, and the Holy Ghost said, "We have created everything in love, and when ADAM sinned, the Son submissively went down on the wing of GABRIEL. And it is for the sake of MARY that the whole universe hath been created." When he saith "for the sake of MARY" it meaneth that the smallest thing shall never be destroyed in the heavens. And MARY carried in her womb the Sun of righteousness (or, justice) and brought Him forth. And when He was brought forth, He was circumcised on the eighth day, according to the 'ÔRÎT, and on the fortieth [Fol. 41b, col. 2] day SIMEON received Him [in his arms]. SIMEON, the priest, continued for many years to hope for the coming of the Lord. Long ago when he was copying the Book of ISAIAH, the prophet, he had found [the passage] which said, "Behold, a virgin shall conceive and bring forth a son", and he said, "Can such a thing as this happen?" Then he threw down his writing-reed, and said, "How can offspring be obtained without a man? or wheat without seed?" And the Holy Spirit told him that he should not die without seeing the Messiah.

82

St. Peter explains the Incarnation

'And three hundred years passed before he saw the Messiah. And when he saw the Child he said, "Now dismiss thy servant", and he continued to recite [the passage] to the end thereof. And God said unto him, "Say unto those who are in SHEOL, 'Your salvation hath drawn nigh, in My own hand I hold it, the Saviour of the world hath come.'" And the Prophets also [rejoiced] [Fol. 42a, col. 1], even as the Lord said, "Joy hath come among the Prophets." And they all were moved so that there might come to pass the word of the prophet who said, "The mountains shall quake in their depths." And straightway ADAM cried out with joy, NOAH leaped with gladness, and ABRAHAM, ISAAC, and JACOB rejoiced. MOSES, and AARON, and JOSHUA offered prayers of thanksgiving, and DAVID smote the lyre, and JOB was dumbfounded, and SOLOMON sang praises, ISAIAH jumped [in the air], JEREMIAH danced, EZEKIEL and DANIEL clapped their hands together, TOBIT stamped with his feet, EZRA was astounded, HOSEA composed hymns of praise, AMOS magnified [God], JOEL called on the Name of the Most High, and MICAH called on the Name of the Merciful [God]. The other Prophets gave thanks, each in his own way, and they went back to their habitations. Some went back to the east, and some went back [Fol. 42a, col. 2] to the west, and some to the north, and some to the south.'

[THE TREES OF PARADISE]

And similarly among the trees in the Garden, there were four kinds: Those which were towards the west were called 'Prophets'; those which were towards the east were called 'Apostles'; those which were towards the north were called 'Priests, Monks, and Martyrs', and those that were to the south were called 'ABRAHAM, ISAAC, JACOB, MOSES, DAVID', and the children with them.

[THE TREE ON WHICH CHRIST WAS CRUCIFIED]

Thou wilt say, 'Whence came the tree whereon they crucified our

Lord?' Did it not come from the Garden (Paradise), and did not an eagle bring it and cast it into JERUSALEM? And this tree was not like (*or*, equal to) the [other] trees. And the trees which were among the highest trees wished that [the JEWS] would crucify our Lord on it, and among the short trees it was the shortest, and it was not equal to them [in height] originally, and it only became so by the crucifixion of our Lord [Fol. 42*b*, col. 1]. And JUDAS ISCARIOT brought it to our Lord for the Crucifixion. This man had sinned the sin of fornication with his mother, he had slain his father with his own hand, and he had stoned his sister to death. Even his ancestor refused [his] blessing; people cried out his name [with curses?]. And when a prophet came into their borders all ISRAEL received a blessing, but he alone received no blessing so that the word of DAVID might come to pass, who said, 'He hath refused the blessing and it removed itself from him', and the children of ISRAEL cursed him because there was not in him what cometh from blessing.

[THE FORMS OF CHRIST AFTER THE RESURRECTION]

The Lord being dead, He rose in His power, and at His Ascension He appointed priests, the Apostles, and He ordained mysteries for them. He appeared to PETER in a form (*or*, symbol) of mystery, and when PETER saw Him as a flame of fire he fled and fell down upon JOHN. To JOHN [Fol. 42*b*, col. 2] He appeared in the form of a white crystal, for he was a virgin. To JAMES He appeared in the form of a sword, for by means of a sword he was to fulfil his martyrdom. To PHILIP He appeared in the form of a lake (*or*, sea). To BARTHOLOMEW He appeared as a vine (*or*, vineyard). To THOMAS He appeared in the form of a bull, for THOMAS had a faith which was like unto strong brass. To MATTHEW He appeared in the form of a babe. To THADDEUS He appeared in the form of an ear of wheat. To NATHANIEL He appeared in the form of a white dove. To JAMES, the son of ALPHAEUS, He appeared in the form of lightning. And after all these things He held converse with them, and said unto them, 'Fear ye not, I am He. Now do ye know your helplessness?' And they were smitten with trembling, and were unable to talk to Him, and they all became like dead men. And He answered them [Fol. 43*a*, col. 1] and said unto them, 'Was it not on the afternoon of the fifth day that I gave My Body and My Blood for you? On this occasion have I not appeared unto you in this form? But ponder and know ye that ye are flesh and blood.' And He said unto PETER, 'If My Body had not appeared in the form of a wheaten loaf, no one would have had the power to receive it.' And having said this He took the bread of His holy Body, and He, the Lord of everything, ascended into heaven. And the Lord said unto PETER, 'Of all sins the greatest are doubt and false dealing, and the counsel of violence and iniquity, and even if a man hath performed just dealing, or hath been a [true] worshipper [of God], or hath kept himself wholly from the doing of things which are banned by religion, if he hath not on his face the mark (*or*, sign) of charitableness, the angel watchers will prevent him from entering into [Fol. 43*a*, col. 2] the gates of heaven.

[THE ABODE OF SOULS]

Now when souls go forth from their bodies where do they dwell? In the earth of their creation, even as ENOCH saith, 'I have seen souls and four places, for there are four gates of heaven, which are DABRA ṢEYÔN, and DABRA ṢEBÂḤ, which is DABRA ZAYT, and DABRA SÎNÂ, and DABRA TÂBÔR. And these [souls] dwell there for one day, and then they stand before the Creator. According to the hour wherein they went forth [from their bodies] the souls of the Christians stand there [for a whole day]. Those who have love in them their city is built with love. Now this I will tell thee, said the angel who was sent unto me, what is the greatest of all are the sufferings of our

Lord on the Cross. He who had brought the world [into being] out of nothing they brought before the assembly of the judges [Fol. 43*b*, col. 1] that they might crucify Him. And He who in the twinkling of an eye could have overwhelmed those who were crucifying Him suffered patiently crucifixion. And they spat in His face, they hurled themselves on Him, they smote Him with blows, they pierced His right side with a spear, and drove nails through His hands and His feet. And when the angels of heaven saw the nakedness of the Lord, they wept, and uttered cries of lamentation, and having grasped their swords, they descended and wanted to slay the whole world. And the Most High, who is filled with long-suffering and abundant mercy, restrained them, saying, 'Destroy not [My] creation, is it not for the sake of My creation that I suffer?'

[The angels] having heard said, 'Glory be unto Thee, O Thou of perpetual mercy and spirit.' Then the angels of the tribe of MICHAEL took their crowns down [from their heads] and they [therewith] the nails [Fol. 43*b*, col. 2] of His right hand. And the [angels of] the tribe of GABRIEL covered the nails in His left foot. And the [angels of] the tribe of 'ÛRÂ'ÊL covered the rent in His side. And the SERÂ-PHÎM overshadowed His head, and the CHERÛBÎM covered His face. And 'ÛRÂ'ÊL and RÛPHÂ'ÊL also covered His face, but no one could cover over wholly Him whose Godhead filled everything. And it is He who covereth the nakedness of face of every created being. Praise and glory be to Him.

[THE ANGEL OF DEATH]

On the day of His Passion, the Angel of Death was plundered. But his power was stripped from him before that, viz. on the first day of the month of ṬEḴEMṬ when He said, 'Ye shall not make the house of thy Father a house of trafficking' (John ii. 16). From that [day] his power was plucked from him, and from that day to His crucifixion was five hundred and forty-five days. And this [number] is not in accordance with the days which have been counted to it, but it must be doubled by thee.

[THE VISION OF CHRIST SEEN BY ALL THE SAINTS]

Our Lord, being dead, rose again [Fol. 44*a*, col. 1] by His own power. And He did not burst the stone which sealed [His tomb], and when He was born He did not violate the virginity of the Virgin. Glory be to Him! He is able to do everything, and there is nothing which is too difficult for Him. The saints have seen the vision of Him, each in his own time, and the vision will not cease until the end of the world. The earliest and the latest prophets have seen the vision.

[THE BEASTS SEEN BY DANIEL]

DANIEL also saw the beasts which went up from the sea through a blast of wind (Daniel vii. 4–7). He saith: The first was like unto a lioness; she had wings and her wings were like unto those of an eagle. I looked until her wings were plucked away, and she rose up and stood upon the feet of a man, and the breast of a man was given to her. And I spake unto her thus: 'Rise up and devour much flesh.'

[THE EXPLANATION]

Behold the explanation: This beast must be interpreted as NEBUCHADNEZZAR [Fol. 44*a*, col. 2], and the lion also of which he speaketh, for the kings of the peoples are called lions. JEREMIAH saith, 'The sheep which was lost the lions have eaten' (Jeremiah xxvii. 17). Now the sheep is the house of ISRAEL. And that he saith, 'I looked until her wings were plucked away' meaneth that his (i.e. NEBUCHADNEZZAR'S) kingdom was plucked away from him. 'She stood upon the feet of a man' showeth that he became a beast through his pride, and that he became a man again, and the heart of a man was given to him. And 'he devoured flesh' meaneth that he ruled over many [lands and peoples].

[DANIEL AND ALEXANDER THE GREAT]

The second beast of which he (i.e. DANIEL) speaketh, a leopard, was ALEXANDER, the son of PHILIP, who was of the seed of JAPHET. The four wings of a bird which, he saith ALEXANDER had, were the four generals of ALEXANDER. The four heads of which he speaketh were the four kingdoms over which the family of ALEXANDER reigned. And the beast which was, he saith, like a bear is DARIUS. He saith that he was like a bear [Fol. 44*b*, col. 1] because the bear is produced by two kinds of animals. His father is the leopard and his mother a wolf. The father of DARIUS was a MENDÊNÂWÊ (i.e. MEDE), of the kings of JAPHET, and his mother [was descended] from the kings of EGYPT.

The last animal which I saw, saith DANIEL, was a horrible beast in the kingdom of the children of ESAU. Concerning this the angel spake unto EZRA, saying: [this is] the fourth kingdom which appeared to DANIEL thy brother; and the children of ESAU shall reign in ROME, and in ZABÎD, and in SELDEN, and in EGYPT. They shall not reign for ever, for the greater number of them shall reign each in succession, one family (i.e. dynasty) after the other. It is for this reason that DANIEL saith, 'mingled among the seed of the children of men.'

[THE EAGLE SEEN BY EZRA]

Now, the explanation of the eagle which EZRA saw (4 Esdras xi. 1–8) is as follows: [Fol. 44*b*, col. 2] The eagle is the kingdom of the children of ESAU, and again it may be interpreted as the False Messiah. For the mother of the False Messiah shall be of the house of ESAU, and therefore he shall be counted with his mother. And see now, the sea is the world, and his three horns are the three kings who reigned before him, and these things shall be completed in the tenth cycle. These are their names: YÂDÎN, KAMADÎN, LAFADÎN. The twelve wings of the eagle of which he speaketh are twelve kings whose names are as follows: YÂBÎBÎN, KÂTÎ, SAʿÂDÎ, HÔDÎ, MÂDÎ, ḤADÎ, DÂDÎ, GÂDÎ, SÂDÎ, NÎDÎ, ʾADÎ, LAWDÎ; these things shall be completed (i.e. fulfilled) in twelve cycles. And when he saith, 'He shall fly with his wings in all the earth', he meaneth that [the King] said to every man, 'Bow down and worship my image' [Fol. 45a, col. 1]. The clouds which, as he saith, shall gather together over him are ENOCH and ELIJAH. The winds of which he speaketh are the righteous, and the heads and little wings of which he speaketh are kings who shall rise up, each in his time. When he saith, 'He hath reduced to subjection to him whatsoever is under the heavens', he meaneth he will give everything into his power, even as the Scriptures have said. When he saith, 'Do not all of you keep watch?', that is, Do not all of you perform justice? And thus he saith to his rulers, 'Ye shall all reign, and ye shall rule after me, each man for one thousand years.'

[CONCERNING ANTICHRIST]

O thou of the false name, who hath taught thee falsehood of such a kind! Of old, even like thyself, MAḤAMAD said, 'After the resurrection of the dead one man shall marry a thousand women.' And he who saith that each man shall reign [Fol. 45a, col. 2] a thousand years is a liar; and in like manner he who saith that one man shall marry a thousand women is a liar.

In that he saith, 'He shall go forth not from his head but from the middle of his body' (4 Esdras xi. 10), this meaneth that he shall be born of the female line of the house of ESAU. And in that he saith, 'eight kings whose years shall be evil', he meaneth [the eight kings] whose names are as follows: NÂDÎ, ṢÂDÎ, ḤALḲADÎ, SÂḤWADÎ, ʾABÂDÎ, ʾASRÂDÎ, ḤAMADÎ, ʾARÔDÎ, who shall die by the hand of a king of the orthodox faith. And when he dieth there shall remain of the thirteen cycles, one hundred years minus three [years] and three weeks which shall be added thereto. And these shall reign each for the period allotted to him. And after them kings shall rise up, each in his own period in ROME, and in [Fol. 45*b*, col. 1] the country of SAʿÂLADÎN whom they shall call 'Tyrant' (*or*, 'Rebel'). But the men of the orthodox faith who have been created kings in ETHIOPIA shall put him to death.

Now all these things did the angel declare before they came to pass to the blessed man BAṢALÔTA MÎKÂ'ÊL. As concerning the three kings of which he speaketh they [shall reign] one hundred years before the ending of the kings who shall rise up with the False Messiah, and he shall be the third of them. And he saith unto thee openly, 'They shall die through a spear-thrust from thee in the fight, and one shall die in his bed.' He saith, 'being mortally wounded', that is the False Messiah who shall be mortally wounded by the knife (*or*, sword) of God. 'The lion which shall rise up from the desert' is the Son; [from the desert] is 'from the peoples' [Fol. 45*b*, col. 2]. And as ISAIAH saith, 'And the peoples shall cry out—the trees of the desert' (Isaiah lv. 12). And SOLOMON saith to the Church, 'Rise up, and go up from the desert', that is to say 'from the peoples'. And DAVID saith, 'The desert shall rejoice and all that therein is' (Psalm xcv. 12), that is to say, the peoples shall rejoice. And those who remain, My people, I will make to rejoice, that is until the day of judgement shall be ended.

[THE DAY OF JUDGEMENT]

That he speaketh thus is because the day of judgement will have the length of one thousand years. Then will the [joy of] those who rejoice come to pass, and whilst they are rejoicing the sinners will be disputing with each other. Blessed indeed will be those who have

believed in CHRIST. If the sin of the believer be as large as a mountain and very great, and if his justice (*or*, just dealing) be only as
large as a spark, that little just dealing [Fol. 46*a*, col. 1] will make
him victorious and do away from him all his sins. Praise and glory
be to Him who hath given faith to him whom He loveth, and want
of faith to him whom He hateth. All those who say, 'The Christians
of the orthodox faith shall be destroyed' are apart from CHRIST.
And if they are called Christians, and have kept the ordinance of
justice, the judgement is not able to look upon them (i.e. harm them).

[THE APOSTLES AND DIVISION OF THE WORLD]

When the Apostles were about to divide the regions of the world
[among them], PETER said, 'Every man who is not a believer shall
not be justified; [that] is what I say (*or*, that is my word) and shall
teach.' And ANDREW said, 'He who hath not been taught [the faith]
shall not be justified; [that] is what I say and shall teach.' And
JAMES said, 'He who shall not be cut in pieces(?) for God's sake,
shall not be justified; [that] is what I say and shall teach' [Fol. 46*a*,
col. 2]. And JOHN said, 'He who is not pure in virginity shall not
be justified; [that] is what I say and shall teach.' And PHILIP said,
'He who hath sworn an oath falsely shall not be justified; [that] is
what I say and shall teach.' And BARTHOLOMEW said, 'He who hath
not honoured his father and his mother shall not be justified; [that]
is what I say and shall teach.' And THOMAS said, 'He who hath not
been slain like a cow (*or*, ox) shall not be justified; [that] is what I say
and shall teach.' And MATTHEW said, 'He who is not as simple (*or*,
innocent) as a dove shall not be justified; [that] is what I say and
shall teach.' THADDEUS said, 'He who is not jealous for the Law
shall not be justified; [that] is what I say and shall teach.' And
NATHANIEL said, 'He who shall not make his body to suffer pain on
the wood of the cross shall not be justified; [that] is what I say and

shall teach.' And JAMES, the son of ALPHAEUS, said, 'He who hath not suffered the pain of stoning [Fol. 46*b*, col. 1] shall not be justified; [that] is what I say and shall teach.' And MATHIAS said, 'He who hath not reduced himself to poverty shall not be justified; [that] is what I say and shall teach.'

And after all the Apostles had spoken in this fashion, PAUL answered and said unto them, 'Hearken ye to me, O my brethren; in this wise is my word [which] I shall teach. He who hath believed and hath been baptized shall be saved, and he who doth not believe shall be condemned. And he who doth not show love to his neighbour shall not be justified; and he who hateth his neighbour shall suffer punishment. In this wise I speak and shall teach.'

[OUR LORD ADDRESSES THE DISCIPLES]

And after the Apostles had spoken in this manner our Lord JESUS CHRIST came. And He said unto them, 'Peace be with you, O My disciples.' And they rose up and bowed down before Him, and they knew that He was our Lord [Fol. 46*b*, col. 2]. And He said unto them, 'What talk did ye talk yesterday? Assuredly I am more pleased with the words of PAUL, My chosen one, and his words delighted me more than all yours. Do I not say in the Gospel, He who hath believed and hath been baptized shall be saved, and he who doth not believe shall be judged (i.e. condemned). With what work can a man be saved if he hath not in him the Faith, and love, and belief? This is far better than becoming a martyr. There is no man who is entirely free from blemish. It is God only who is absolutely perfect. And [certainly] ye are men. Look at the heavens and they [even] are not pure before me.

'Thou PETER didst deny me thrice in a night, and I have forgiven thee thy sin, although there is no sin which is greater [Fol. 47*a*, col. 1] than the denial of the Creator.

92

'And thou JOHN whilst I was being crucified didst make thyself happy with the high priests.

'And thou ANDREW didst go forth for ḤEQUÂ(?).

'And thou JAMES did abandon thine apparel and didst flee.

'And thou PHILIP didst go forth into the middle of the city.

'And thou BARTHOLOMEW, with RÂKÛB, thy sister's son, didst disappear.

'And thou THOMAS didst drive away on a chariot, and made thyself to disappear.

'And thou MATTHEW didst hide thyself in the city, and didst go forth therefrom secretly by night.

'And thou THADDEUS didst muffle thyself in a cloak and go forth.

'And thou NATHANIEL didst hide thyself under a *dûr*.

'And thou, JAMES, the son of ALPHAEUS, didst hide thyself underground in a field.

'Thus have ye done [Fol. 47a, col. 2], and I have not abandoned you, nay, on the contrary, I have chosen you and appointed you to be my heirs.'

[THE DECISION OF THE APOSTLES AFTER THE ASCENSION]

And after the Ascension of our Lord the Apostles said, 'It is meet that we should die for the Name of CHRIST our God.' And the martyrs came one after the other, and they said, 'Let us hand over our souls for the sake of the Name of CHRIST, our God.' And after all [the marty]rs came the monks, for with them is planted the reward which is perfect (*or*, complete). This is the work and spiritual excellence, of ANTHONY, the head of the monks. Among men there is no one who hath fought the fight of spiritual life so strenuously as ANTHONY. His father in the world was an exceedingly rich man, and was the owner of five hundred yoke of oxen. Whilst his father dwelt thus he died, after the manner of every man [Fol. 47b, col. 2].

The Temptations of St. Anthony

And ANTHONY said, 'What hath happened to thee, [O] father? And where is thy voice wherewith thou didst command thy slaves? And nothing hath harmed thee except that the little breath which thou didst breathe hath failed and is not with thee.' And having said these words ANTHONY went out into the desert; now he was at that time eighteen years of age. And ANTHONY was tempted on twelve [important] occasions, and the other temptations which he suffered were numberless. ANTHONY shone with light which was twelve times stronger than that of the sun, whilst the light of the saints is only seven times brighter than the light of the sun. And some shine with the light of the moon and some with light like the stars.

[THE TEMPTATIONS OF ST. ANTHONY]

[Now consider] the following examples of the spiritual endurance of ANTHONY. [He was tempted] first of all by a woman. Secondly by the ARABS; thirdly by the devils when they made him to come down from the mountain thirty times; fourthly by hunger; fifthly by thirst for water; [Fol. 47*b*, col. 2] sixthly by the wild animals; seventhly by the sword; eighthly by the thrust of a spear when he was speared by wicked men; ninthly by the [attacks of] the *'anḳâl*, that is to say lice (*or*, mosquitoes); tenthly by the words [which he heard] saying, 'Get thee back to the world'; eleventhly by the buffetings of men; and twelfthly by [the attacks of] the baboons(?). And these saints vanquished SATAN, bearing in mind that the world was transient.

[THE COMING OF OUR LORD AND ANTICHRIST]

And the man of God asked the angel who had been sent unto him, and said unto him, 'What is going to take place at the end of the world?' And the angel said unto him, 'There shall reign a king, a man of iniquity, even as the Scriptures say. And JOHN of the

The Coming of Antichrist

Apocalypse saith, 'The Lord shall come mounted on a white horse' (Revelation xix. 11). The work of the False [CHRIST] will be thus: He will come forth [Fol. 48a, col. 1] having torn the womb of his mother, and he will kill his father, and he will sit upon a throne and will reign. And when the days of his reign are fulfilled, our Lord will come with His army. First of all ELIJAH the TISHBITE will strike a blow on his chest, JOSHUA, the son of NUN, will smite him on the forehand, and DAVID, the harpist, will spear him in the bowels, and PETER will spear his horse, and THEODORE and CLAUDIUS will break open his armour and will cut off his head, and JOHN will spear his horse again. And there will be [heard] a mighty voice which will say, 'I have killed, and I made haste.' And the fire of the anger going forth from the mouth of the Lord shall kill him, and his army shall die with him. And ELIJAH shall bind on a tiara of gold [Fol. 48a, col. 2], and JOSHUA shall put on a garment of green-gold brocade(?), and PETER a . . . of gold, and JOHN a white . . . , and THEODORE and CLAUDIUS red crowns, and DAVID and the other saints fillets(?) of gold.

And after this the Resurrection and the Judgement(?) shall take place. And there shall be spread out for the chosen ones the heavens wherewith God hath enveloped His throne like a secret letter. And this earth shall be a . . . trodden by the foot of a just (or, righteous) man. Then there shall be a new heaven and a new earth, and the Garden (i.e. Paradise) shall appear. And the trees of Paradise, when they bring forth fruit shall produce men. When he saith, 'When they bring forth fruit', the meaning is when they bring forth good works [Fol. 48b, col. 1]. The man who teacheth one word in the Psalms of DAVID, that [word] shall bring forth each day ten thousand fruits. Reveal not this word of mystery to any except those who are learned (i.e. the doctors); hide and reveal not that which is from God. He who hath chosen the word of God is worth more than gold and silver. For everything which is of the flesh is

95

End of the Book of Mystery

like the grass, and everything of honour is like the fruit of the grass. And the word of God abideth for ever.

The Book of Mystery is ended. And if it be read it will produce wonderment. He who heareth this book will be astounded, and it will make the heart of a man to shine like the brilliant sun.

PART II

> Here VANSLEB's copy does not agree with PEIRESC's manuscript, and there are mistakes in the readings of both. The latter reads:
>
> አይሰ ፡ በየ ፡ መድየ ፡ የቤ፹ ፡ ደ፹ ፡ ወ፯
>
> Here we have the letters of a name A. Y. S. M. Y. D. W(?) ... which suggests 'ASMODEUS', but the total of the numbers which are assigned to each letter make less than the number 666, thus 100+3+200+30+

97

O

30+6. But if we read ሰሤ for ሰሮ, and ፈቧሿ for ፈቧሿ we get 100+ 300+200+30+30+6 = 666.

VANSLEB's copy reads [Fol. 88a, col. 2]

አሤ : ሰሮ : መሤ : ፈቧሿ : ፈሿ : ወኽ,

i.e. 200+3+200+30+30+6 = 469.

Even if we read ሰሤ, i.e. S = 300, instead of ሰሮ, we obtain the number 766. It is clear that both the scribe who wrote PEIRESC's manuscript and VANSLEB made a mistake in reckoning the numbers attached to the name of ASMEDAI or ASMODEUS.

The acrostic name 'ASMYÂDÎ is made up of the initial letters of the names of 'the captains of the army of SATAN,' thus:

A stands for '*Agânenet*, i.e. 'Devils'. S stands for SATAN. M stands for MÂSTÊMÂ. YÂ stands for YEY. [BÊ stands for BÊLḤÔR.] DÎ stands for DÎYABLÔS (DIABOLUS).[1]

The three angels of the Apocalypse were JOHN the Baptist, the Son of God, and PETER.

The sea of glass a symbol of the saints.

The Seven Vials were Seven Prophets, viz. MOSES, JOSHUA, SAMUEL, ELIJAH, ISAIAH, EZEKIEL, and JOHN the Baptist.

The Twelve Stones chosen by JOSHUA are the Twelve Apostles.

List of the Kings whose names are written in the Book of CLEMENT.

The False CHRIST, a king of TÊMÂN who was like an ox.

List of the Books of the New Testament.

The book of MOSES which was carried up into heaven by an angel.

The blessings which shall come upon the readers of this Book.

[Fol. 48a, col. 1, l. 19]. A DISCOURSE AND A NARRATIVE OF LIFE, [viz.] THE INTERPRETATION OF THE APOCALYPSE OF JOHN [made to] his colleague (i.e. BAKHAYLA MÎKÂ'ÊL) which he wrote down as a foundation of the Gospel of Divinity [Fol. 48b, col. 2]. It shall serve me as a guide (*or*, rudder) of righteousness (*or*, justification) whithersoever I shall go.

---

[1] According to Mr. L. H. Gray (*Journal Royal Asiatic Society*, October, 1934, p. 792, the name Asmodeus probably means 'Sky-demon', and he was none other than Ahuramazda, thus the god pure and simple.

The Burial of Moses

In the Name of the Holy Trinity I spake and asked questions concerning the mysteries of God. The blessed Father Abbâ zôsî-MÂS, that is to say, BAKHAYLA MÎKÂ'ÊL, saith: I stood up for forty days and forty nights in an abyss of water, even as (i.e. the same time as) MOSES fasted. And then again JOHN fasted[1] exceedingly, and he read(?) the Gospel which had been previously told him, until at length he spake; and this took place through the life which was in him. And another angel spake and said, 'There was a certain man who was sent from God, and his name was JOHN' (John i. 6).

[THE BURIAL OF MOSES]

And MOSES [fasted] forty days and forty nights, and every Friday he used to take sheets of cloth for his funeral shroud and sew them together [ready] for [Fol. 49a, col. 1] the day of his death. And according to what God said unto him in the mountains, one day he met (or, found) two angels who were digging a grave; GABRIEL was one and MICHAEL was the other. And MOSES said unto them, 'May God give you help!' And the angels said unto him, 'Show us a favour. Come and show us our measure for the grave [by lying down in it].' And when MOSES measured it by lying down therein, they covered him over with earth and left him therein. And they cried out and said, 'We have buried the man of God.' And when they were saying this they were standing among a crowd of people. And the people ran up the hill into the mountain, and they were unable to find the place wherein MOSES had been buried.

[JOHN THE VIRGIN EXPLAINS HIS BOOK OF THE APOCALYPSE]

And this (i.e. the following) was the Word [which came] after I spake. JOHN the Virgin came to me, and he showed me the Book

[1] Moses fasted forty days and nights and wrote the Law; John fasted for long periods and wrote the Apocalypse; Bakhayla Mîkâ'êl stood in water forty days and nights and then wrote the present work.

which gave him knowledge, and he began to declare unto me the interpretation of the Book of his Vision.

[THE SEVEN CHURCHES]

And he told me that when he says 'Seven Churches' [Fol. 49a, col. 2] he means the Seven Churches which the Apostles established at their first preaching.

And the name of the angel of the Church of the EPHESIANS is DAMATRU. And in that he holdeth seven stars in his right hand, the stars whereof he speaketh represent the seven angels [of the Seven Churches] and the seven lamps (or, candlesticks) of gold are the Seven Churches (Rev. i. 20).

And the name of the angel of the SARDÎNÔN (SARDINIANS) (Rev. iii. 1) was ṬABÂDEN (?), and he is [on] the throne of PETER. And I said unto him, 'Who is he that was cast into prison?' (Acts v. 18). And he said unto me, 'It was PETER my brother.' And that he saith, 'They suffered ten days', that meaneth the ten days which the Apostles fasted after He had ascended into heaven.

And [I asked], 'What is the name of the angel of PERGAMÔN?' (Rev. ii. 18). And the Apostle answered and said unto me, 'His name is 'ÎYÂSÛ.'

And [I asked], 'What is the name of the angel of TÎYÂ ṬEREN?' (THYATIRA) (Rev. ii. 18). And the angel said unto me [Fol. 49a, col. 1], 'DÎGÎBÂ'ÊL is his name.'

And again I said, 'What is the name of the angel of the SARDÎSÂN [*sic*]? And the Apostle said unto me, 'PHÛBÊRÊN is his name.'

And [again] I said, 'What is the name of the angel of PHILA-DELPHIA?' (Acts iii. 7). And the Apostle said unto me, 'REKHÊ'ÊL is his name, and he is the second SEM'ÂN (SIMON).' And there is a door which is opened and no one is able to close it; what he saith meaneth baptism.

The Seven Seals. The Seven Books of the Church

And again I said, 'What is the name of the angel of LAODICEA?'
(Acts iii. 14). And [the Apostle] said unto me, 'GABRIEL THEOLOGUS
is his name.'

And [the Apostle] said unto me, 'Understand, and hearken to
a mystery which I will tell thee; hearken as one who is obedient.'
And he said, 'These seven who have been named [are given] the
names by which they were called before they were Apostles.'

[THE SEVEN SEALS]

The word of JOHN 'ABÛ ḴALAMSÎS[1] (i.e. JOHN of the Apocalypse):

He saw a Book and the Seven Seals thereof. Now the Book is
ADAM [Fol. 49b, col. 2], and the Seven Seals are the things which
He gave to ADAM, viz. (1) sovereignty, (2) priesthood, (3) prophecy,
(4) authority as judge, (5) governorship, (6) the true Faith, (7) cere-
monial purity. When he saith that the opener of the seals thereof
was God, he meaneth the creation of man and everything which
appertaineth to man. Observe thou that he speaketh unto thee
openly (or, clearly), 'I have been killed for [him] and I have poured
out over him my blood'. Now for whom would He have shed His
blood except ADAM? Concerning the Seven Seals he speaketh
what he interpreteth.

[THE SEVEN BOOKS OF THE CHURCH]

And the Lamb (Rev. v. 6) of whom he speaketh is the Son. As to
the seven horns and seven eyes—the horns are the Archbishops,
and the Bishops, and the priests, and the deacons, and the readers;
and the seven eyes (Rev. v. 6) which he mentioneth are the Seven
Books of the Church. The first is the [Fol. 50a, col. 1] complete
Evangeliarium. The second [is the Book of] the Apostles who sent
forth their messengers. The third is the Acts of the Apostles. The
fourth is the Book of the Epistles of PAUL in its entirety. The fifth

[1] Literally 'Father of Ḵalamsîs' (Apocalypse).

101

The Interpretation of the Seven Seals

is the Book of Synods in its entirety. The sixth is the Book of the Apocalypse which [JOHN] saw. The seventh is the Book of the Covenant, and the DIDASKALIA, arranged together. This is what the angel of God declared and interpreted.

[THE SEVEN SEALS INTERPRETED] [Rev. vi.]

The first seal of which he speaketh is the primeval time of the world. And there went out a white horse, that is to say ADAM, and he who was mounted upon him was CHRIST, who put on the flesh of man. The bow which he says he made strong was the bow of the Cross of the Only One, even as JOB saith, 'I will go forward my bow being in my hand' (Job xxix. 20?). And again [Fol. 50a, col. 2] he saith thus in the Gospel: 'And they took Him, and thrust Him outside [the city], and they dragged Him as they carried His Cross' (Matt. xxvii. 24–34). And as to what he saith, 'They gave Him a crown of thorns, and He went forth that He might conquer', this speech of his meaneth that mortal flesh conquered SATAN.

And the second horse of which he speaketh (Rev. vi. 4), which went forth is NOAH. And when he saith 'red' he is alluding to the blood and slaying which took place in the days of NOAH (Rev. vi. 5).

And with the [breaking of] the third seal a black horse went forth, he is speaking of the worship of idols.

As to the measure of wheat for a *dînâr* of which he speaketh, the *dînâr* is the Faith (Rev. vi. 6), and the wheat is the flesh of our Lord. And as to the wine and the oil which, he saith, did not dry up, the wine is the blood of our Lord, and the oil is baptism. And there [Fol. 50b, col. 1] are the things which shall never be lacking until the destruction of the world.

And at the [breaking of] the fourth seal, there went forth a green horse (Rev. vi. 8), and this horse of which he speaketh is the Holy 'ÔRÎT (i.e. the TÔRÂH, the Hebrew LAW), and the name of him who rode him was DEATH. The 'ÔRÎT of which he speaketh saith, 'He who killeth, they (i.e. the people) shall kill him' (Deut. xix. 6, 12). But the Gospel saith, 'To him that smiteth thee on thy cheek turn to him the other [that he may smite it also]' (Luke vi. 29). And to this ruling what are we to say? The Gospel is life, and is the food of the spirit, but the food of the body is bread, and the food of the spirit is the word of the spirit.

And at the [breaking of] the fifth seal (Rev. vi. 9) what JOHN saw under the altar were the souls of those who had been killed for the word of God; these were the Prophets who had been killed in the fifth [Fol. 50*b*, col. 2] period.

And at the [breaking of] the sixth seal (Rev. vi. 12) there was an earthquake. That about which he speaketh took place at the time of the Crucifixion of our Lord (Matt. xxiv. 7; xxvii. 54). And as the Gospel saith, 'The earth quaked, and the rocks were split asunder, and the blood poured down and entered into the mouth of ADAM.' And as to what he saith, 'the sun went black' (Rev. vi. 12); the Gospel saith that the sun went black from the sixth until the ninth hour. And the stars that fell from heaven of which he speaketh were the people of ISRAEL.

And when he opened the seventh seal (Rev. viii. 1) everything which was in heaven and upon the earth remained silent (i.e. motionless) for half an hour; the silence of which he speaketh concerneth the end of the world, even as EZRA saith, 'He shall make the earth silent for seven days.' This is what he meaneth when he saith, 'The world shall be consumed [Fol. 51*a*, col. 1] and shall be silent seven days.'

[THE ANGELS AND THE TRUMPETS] [Rev. viii]

Here is a word of mystery of 'ABÛ ḲALAMSÎS:

When the first angel blew the trumpet (Rev. viii. 7) there came

103

hail (*or,* ice) and fire mixed with blood, and it came down into the earth; and this was because of ADAM.

And the second angel who blew the trumpet of whom he speaketh is the second plague. And the hail and fire which descended on the earth is the flood of hail.

And when the third angel blew the trumpet (Rev. viii. 10) a great star came hurtling down, and it was blazing like a fire, and it was SATAN. And that SATAN is called a star, hear from ISAIAH who saith, 'How hath descended the star of the morning wrenched [from heaven]!' (Isaiah xiv. 12). And it descended upon the third part of the rivers. The rivers of which he speaketh are the prophets, and the springs (*or,* fountains) of waters are the children [Fol. 51*a*, col. 2] of the prophets. And the wormwood is SATAN (Rev. viii. 11), for all the doctrine of SATAN is bitterness, and the end of him leadeth down to perdition.

[A STATEMENT AND A DISCOURSE OF MYSTERY(?) OF 'ABÛ ḴALAMSÎS]

And at the blast of the trumpet of the fourth angel (Rev. viii. 12) the sun became shrouded and went black, that is to say, three parts thereof, and three parts of the moon, and [three parts of] the day and the night likewise. The interpreter whom God sent saith, 'The sun was obscured', and this hath reference to the HEBREWS from PHARAOH. For he compareth the HEBREWS to the sun because of their own Faith, and because of the firm Faith of their fathers. And as concerning the 'one third of it which went black', and of which he speaketh [Fol. 51*b*, col. 1] it hath reference to the thirty thousand children who died in ISRAEL in one day at the weeping of RACHEL. Now, RACHEL was the wife of a priest. And when they were oppressed by the work of making bricks, and the bringing forth of their twin(?) children, she made a child in mud brick, and she cried out saying, 'Is 'ÎYÂSÛS in heaven?' Then straightway did God come down on Mount sînâ, and He spake unto MOSES and said unto him, 'Assuredly I have heard the groaning of my people, and I have come down to deliver them' (Exod. ii. 24; vi. 5). And again, this is a word of mystery.

And when the fifth angel blew his trumpet (Rev. ix. 1), a great star came down from heaven, and it was like unto a flaming fire [Fol. 51b, col. 2]. And there went up a smoke like unto the smoke of a big furnace, and it covered over the sun; and that smoke was like unto a cloud. And from that dense smoke there went forth locusts on the earth, and he gave them power to become like scorpions on the earth. And he commanded them not to hurt and not to destroy the grass, or any green thing, or any tree, but only the men who had not got the seal of God on their foreheads. He speaketh the interpretation which he declared by the mouth of the Holy Spirit.

The fifth seal is true. The star is JOHN the Baptist unto whom was given the key of baptism. And the smoke is the Spirit [Fol. 52a, col. 1] which came up from the abyss. And the sun is the Only Son, which the Holy Spirit covered after the manner of a cloud. And the Gospel saith unto thee plainly 'a shining cloud came and covered Him' (Luke ix. 34).

And as to the events which came forth from the abyss into the earth, these are the peoples who have received the power to act as priests from the King of the heavens and the earth. And when he says, 'He commanded them not to destroy the grass' (Rev. ix. 3), he meaneth by 'grass' the prophecy of the Prophets, which is called 'grass', even as SOLOMON saith, 'Gather together to thyself the grass of the mountain' (Prov. xxvii. 25 ?). And the green things of which he speaketh are the children of baptism. And those who have not the seal of the Creator on [Fol. 52a, col. 2] their foreheads, are the evil doers, and the devils. And the five months of which he speaketh

(Rev. ix. 5) are the five months wherein they shall suffer torture in the furnace of the wicked from the days of the False Messiah. For the waters shall be withdrawn from the face of the earth, and straightway there shall be sore affliction on the earth. Now concerning this he informeth thee openly, saying, 'And in those days a man shall seek for death and shall not find it' (Rev. ix. 6).

THE WORDS OF MYSTERY OF JOHN 'ABÛ ḲALAMSÎS ARE THUS:

The appearance of these locusts is like unto that of horses who are ready to enter into battle. And these are the Christians who fight against SATAN, even as PAUL saith, 'Your fighting is not against flesh and blood [Fol. 52b, col. 1], but against the filthy spirits who cover the world with darkness, that is to say with SATANS' (Ephes. vi. 12). And there is none who can conquer them unless he hath in him humility, and faith, and love. And when SATAN seeth humility in a man he burneth with indignation and becometh like a raging fire. And that this saying is truly so, hear the Gospel which our Lord spake: 'Two men went up into the temple to pray, and the humble man was justified, and the arrogant man was condemned' (Luke xviii. 10). And with them was a king, the angel of the abyss. The abyss of which he speaketh is the Church, and the king is the Son. And the name [of SATAN] in Hebrew is ''ABDÔN,' and in Greek, 'APÔLLYÔN, which showeth [Fol. 52b, col. 2] that the HEBREWS made him a slave (*or*, madman), and 'APÔLLYÔN means, 'the wise one of those who are chosen'.

And in the days of the False Messiah, when water was lacking, men used to crush the needy men, and take and pound up their limbs together in a mortar, and make them into food for the False Messiah. And he would deliver the man [who did this] and shield him from tribulation in that day.

Symbolism of the Seven Earthquakes

[CONCERNING THE APOCRYPHAL BOOKS OF THE OLD LAW]

And concerning the Books which were withdrawn (*or*, apocryphal) from the 'ÔRÎT; [they were] three, even as EZRÂ saith. He said unto MOSES, 'This declare and this withdraw (*or*, hide).' And from DAVID [they were] five, even as he saith. And from ISAIAH [they were] seven, as he himself saith, 'there were others of my words'. And from ZACHARIAS [there was] one, even as he himself saith, 'I saw a knife (*or*, sickle) travelling in the heavens' (Zech. v. 1?), and the sickle [Fol. 53*a*, col. 1] is the Word of God which shall harvest the wicked for punishment, and the chosen ones for life. And from JEREMIAH [there were] three, even as God (*or*, the Lord) saith, 'Hide what is mine, my speech.' And again he saith, 'I will take one from the town and two from the country, and I will carry them into ZION. And I will make them to be governors.'

Behold the interpretation thereof. The one from the town of whom he speaketh, are the ISRAELITES who shall be found in the preaching of the Apostles. And the two from the country of whom he speaketh are the seed of HAM and the seed of JAPHET, who are found in the praise of the Apostles. And from SÎRÂK [there were] two [books] even as he himself saith, 'Until the reason therefore shall be found, hide my word.'

[THE SEVEN EARTHQUAKES OR THUNDERS] [Rev. x]

And concerning the Seven Earthquakes (i.e. Thunders) of which he speaketh in connexion with the seal, these are the Seven Hidden Things which are hidden from men. And some of them are fair (*or*, beautiful) and some are hideous. The FIRST which is hidden from the heart of a man, is Death, even as PAUL saith, 'Behold, hidden is the word which I speak unto you, for we shall all die.' And the SECOND is the Faith which is hidden from the heart of the wicked, even as PAUL himself saith, 'Hidden is our merciful kindness to the wicked.' The THIRD is love. For love being a thing which is beautiful, man seeketh after that which is hateful and licentious(?). And the FOURTH is the fear of God which is not blotted out from the heart of a man. And the FIFTH is the constitution of man (*or, natural disposition*) which is stubborn. And the SIXTH [Fol. 53*b*, col. 1]. From one teat goeth forth milk, and when it is slain (*or, sacrificed*) it becometh blood. And so the calf when it is born: the young creature fleeth to the teat of its mother, and even so is it with a man. And the SEVENTH is the mercy of God which is hidden from the heart of a man, even as God Himself saith, 'My mercy shall not be known unto every one who is [in the] flesh.'

Now behold, I have finished [telling] thee the words of mystery, and it seemeth to me that the following discourse resembleth [these]: Speak thou unto the children of men, saying, 'Thou mayest deny what the Scriptures say, but there is nothing hidden from the Scriptures.' And together with this it may be said, there is nothing which can be desired, and if thou desirest then thou art seeking suffering for thyself. And hear what our Lord saith in the Book of Mystery; now the Book of [Fol. 53*a*, col. 2] Mystery is the Book of the Covenant. He saith, 'Those who sow seed in ground which is unsuitable seek suffering for themselves.' And PAUL saith, 'The man who denieth thou mayest perhaps rebuke once, and then leave him alone, and make him to know that he is a wicked man.' It is better that the word of the wise man should be spoken to the wise, even as PAUL saith, 'Speak words of wisdom to the wise.' And hearken also to the word of the Prophets and Apostles, 'There have gone forth from JACOB and the House of ISRAEL those who are called sheep', even as ENOCH saith, 'From the ass of the desert shall be born an ox', that is to say, ABRAHAM from TÂRÂ, and a ram shall be born [Fol. 54*b*, col. 1] from the ram, which he saith is JACOB, from ISAAC. And ESAU he calls 'a pig of the desert'.

Classification of Nations by Enoch

In this wise doth ENOCH, the prophet, give names to the various peoples. The AMALEKITES eagles, the EGYPTIANS bears(?), the ISHMAELITES wild asses of the desert, the ARABS *'Aṭâlê* (ከጣሴ:), the CANAANITES crows (*or*, ravens), the PHILISTINES wolves, the MOABITES hyraxes, the PERSIANS lions, the AMMONITES scorpions, the MIDIANITES serpents, the SEED OF JAPHET tigers, and the EDOMITES wolves (*or*, foxes). Thus did ENOCH the prophet, who described what was to happen before it took place, give names to each of these nations and define their characteristic qualities.

[THE PROPHETS]

I will now speak about the Prophets. The Apostle related the following to me and said, 'The first of all the Prophets [Fol. 54*a*, col. 1] is ADAM our father, who was from the earth, and his father was God his creator.'

And the father of ENOCH was YÂRÊD and his mother BARÛKA.

And NOAH begot his son MÂTÛSELÂ, the father of LÂMÊKH, and his mother was BÊTÊNÎS. Now he was the prophet who prophesied that a flood of water would come into the world.

And ABRAHAM was the prophet who prophesied many things as the Book KUEFÂLÊ telleth thee. ABRAHAM prophesied, saying, 'Children shall be raised up for the making anew thy Law', and these [children] are the Apostles. And again he saith unto thee, 'There shall be a world of peace' and this was to be because of the Son, for He set peace in the world, even as PAUL saith, 'And He made peace with His Cross', and because ABRAHAM made an offering [Fol. 54*b*, col. 1], God said unto him, 'Take thee an ox of three years, and a kid of three years, and a dove and a turtle dove.' Behold the interpretation of this. ABRAHAM is to be interpreted as the Son, and the ox of three years whereof he speaketh is ADAM, and the three years are the three periods from the year of which he speaketh. For the Nations went forth from the three sons of NOAH, and from the three of them our Lord took the Nations in His preaching of the Gospel. And the dove is MARY, our Lady, and the turtle dove is PAUL the Apostle. 'Ye shall not cut off the birds', he saith, for the birds are the doctors [of the Church] and they shall not be cut off until the end of the world [Fol. 54b, col. 2]. And the turning towards evening of which he speaketh is assuredly the end of the world. Again our Lord saith, 'The time of the turn of the day towards evening hath come' (Luke xxiv. 29); assuredly this is the end of the world. Even as PAUL saith, 'at the end of the world'. At the coming of the end of the world the Son went forth to destroy sin. The flame of fire is the Son, and the furnace is the Cross.

[ABBÂ BAKHAYLA MÎKÂ'ÊL ASKS THE APOSTLE FOR INFORMATION]

Go back now, and tell me how the Prophets arose, and the names of their fathers and their mothers; tell me again, he saith. And the interpreter said, 'ABRAHAM came forth from TÂRÂ, because he was of the seed of SHEM; and the name of his mother was 'ÊWÂS, that is to say, the 'Meek.' And from ABRAHAM there separated a Nation and Nations.

And from [Fol. 55a, col. 1] the seed of JACOB sprang (*or*, sprouted) the Prophets.

And the first prophet in the 'ÔRÎT was MOSES MELKÔM. He and AARON the priest were of the House of LEVI. And the name of their father was 'ENBARÂM, and the name of their mother was YÔKABED; and the name of their sister was MARGÂM.

And 'ÎYÂSÛ (JOSHUA) [whom] they call the son of NÊWÎ (NUN).

SAMUEL was of the house of LÊWÎ of MÎRÂRÎ; and the name of his father was ḤELḲÂNÂ. And the name of his mother was ḤANÂ (HANNAH), and she was descended from the house of ISRAEL.

DAVID the prophet and king. His descent was from the tribe of JUDAH. His father was 'ÊSEY (JESSE), and the name of his mother was ḤEBLÎ'LÊ. He prophesied until the coming of the Son, eighteen hundred years.

SOLOMON [Fol. 55a, col. 2] his son was a prophet, and his mother was BÊRSÂBÊḤ (BATHSHEBA).

And 'ÊLYAS (ELIJAH) was a prophet from the tribe of LÊWÎ.

PHÎNÂHÂS was the son of 'ÊL'ÂZÂR the priest. The name of his father was 'ÎYASÊNYÛ(?), and the name of his mother was BÎTÔNÂ.

And 'ÎYSAYÂS (ISAIAH) was of the tribe of SIMON. And his mother was of the house of RÔBÊL. And the name of his father was 'AMÔS. And the name of [his mother was] 'ARÊNÎS. And he prophesied until the coming of the Beloved seven hundred and sixty-five years.

And 'ÊRMEYÂS (JEREMIAH) was of the tribe of LÊWÎ from ḲA'ÂT. And the name of his father was KÊLKÊYÛ, and the name of his mother was WÊṬÊLÊS. His place of abode was 'ANÂTÔT, in the country of BENYÂM. And moreover the name of his father was MALABÊNÊ. And he prophesied until the coming [Fol. 55b, col. 1] of our Lord.

And DAN'AL (DANIEL) who was of the tribe of JUDAH. And the name of his father was 'ÎYÔAKIM, king of JUDAH. And the name of his mother was MÊLÊNÂS. He prophesied until the coming of the Word (ḲÂL) four hundred and four years.

And the Three Children. The name of their father was SÊMYÛ (LÊMYÛ?), and the name of their mother was NÂTRÎ, and also ḤANNÂ. And the father of DANIEL and the father of the Three Children were brothers.

ḤEZḲE'ÊL (EZEKIEL) was of the tribe of LÊWÎ and ḲA'ÂT. The name of his father was BÛZ and the name of his mother was NÔRÊ. And he prophesied until the coming of the Only One four hundred and sixty-four years.

'EZRA, who was called SÛTÛ'ÊL, was of the tribe of LÊWÎ. His father's name was SÊRYÛ, and the name of his mother was SÂLÔ. He prophesied until the Coming [Fol. 55*b*, col. 2] of the Son five hundred and thirty-seven(?) years.

And ṬÔBÎT was of the house of NAPHTÂLÊM. The name of his father was GEBA'ÊL and the name of his mother was MÊSÊDÊ.

And 'ÎYÂSÛ SÎRÂK was the son of 'AL'ÂZAR the priest, who is SEM'ÂN the priest; and his name was ḤANNÂ.

And HÔSE'A was of the tribe of JOSEPH. And the name of his father was BÊ'ÊREM and the name of his mother was MÊSÊLÊ.

And 'AMÔṢ was of the tribe of SIMEON. And the name of his father was ZÎTÂR and the name of his mother was MÎSÂTÂ. And he was the father of 'ÎSÂYAYÂS the prophet.

And MEKYÂS (MICAH) was of the tribe of BENYÂM, and the name of his father was 'AMDÂ, who is MÛRÂT, and the name of his mother was SATAMÔ, that is to say, SÊTÂNÎ.

And 'IYÛ'ÊL (JOEL) was of the tribe of RÔBÊL (REUBEN), and the name of his father was RÔBÊL, and the name of his mother was MÎSÎRÎ, that is to say [Fol. 56*a*, col. 1], BATU'ÊL.

And 'ABADYÛ (OBADIAH) was of the tribe of EPHRAIM. And the name of his father was KÔKALÂ and the name of his mother was SAPLITÊ.

And JONAH was of the house of ISSACHAR. And the name of his father was 'AMÂTÊ, and the name of his mother was MÂTAL.

And NAHÔM was of the tribe of ZEBULON. And the name of his father was ḤELḲESYÛS, and the name of his mother was 'ANBÎNÂ, who is SÔNÂ.

And 'ENBÂḲÔM (HABAKKUK) was of the tribe of SIMEON. And the name of his father was DAKÔR and the name of his mother was SÛRÂPHA, who is RÂSPHEYÂ, because she was following an announcement of the SÛRÂPHÊM (SERÂPHÎM).

And SAPHÔNYÂS (ZEPHANIAH) was of the tribe of NAPHTÂLÊM. And the name of his father was SÊDÊK, who is the same as GÔTÔLYÂL(?), the AMORITE, and the name of his mother was MÊRÔBÂ, but she was also called NEḤEB. And he was called 'AMORITE' because his inheritance was the land [Fol. 56a, col. 2] of the AMORITES. And ḤAGGÎ was of the tribe of GÂD. And his mother was of the tribe of DÂN. And the name of his father was 'AṬOṬÂ and the name of his mother was LÊNÊ.

And ZAKÂRYÂS was of the tribe of LÊWÎ. And the name of his father was BARÛKÎYÂ, and the name of his mother was ḤÔDÂ. And the name [is] from KHÊWÛ KHALÊ(?).

And MELKEYÂS (MULUCHI) was from the tribe of ASHÊR. And the name of his father was PHÂḤÊL, and the name of his mother was SEGÊNÊ(?).

And GÂD the prophet was of the tribe of DÂN. And the name of his father was MÔṢ, and the name of his mother was NABÎ, which is the same as NABÎL.

And JOHN, the Crown of the Prophets, was of the house of LÊWÎ. And the name of his father was ZAKÂRYÂS, and the name of his mother was ELISABETH.

And to ḤAGGÎ also—the name of his mother was SÔNÂ, which is the same as LÊNÎ.

Such was the origin (*or*, descent) [Fol. 56b, col. 1] of the Prophets from the twelve sons of JACOB. And there is no prophet who did not proceed from JACOB, with the sole exception of JOB, who in this matter may be compared to the Son. Now JOB was of the house of ESAU. And there is no Apostle who did not proceed from JACOB. And EZEKIEL prophesied concerning the Apostles. And concerning the Son he saith, 'He came to a door, and He went out through it, the door remaining shut.' [The door is] MARY the Virgin.

And again EZEKIEL saith, 'I saw six men [with axes] who came from the north, and six men like unto them who came from the east, and each one of them had an axe in his hand. And the interpretation of these twelve men is the Twelve Apostles. And the axe [which each carried] is the Word of God [Fol. 56*b*, col. 2]. And as he saith in the Gospel, 'The axe is laid at the root of the trees' (Matt. iii. 10), and the trees about which he speaketh are men.

And concerning this matter EZEKIEL saith, 'All those who have not the Sign [of the Law] they cut down, and those who have on them the Sign they spare.' The meaning of this is: Those who have in them the belief in the Trinity shall be saved. And those who have not in them the Faith of which he speaketh shall be deprived of his mercy. And of the saints of which he speaketh, the first are ISRAEL, and these, if it be that they have rejected the Faith, shall be [the first] to be cut down.

And ZAKÂRYÂS saith concerning the Son, 'I saw in the night a man who was mounted on a red horse, and he stood between two mountains which were enveloped in shadow [Fol. 57*a*, col. 1]. And behind him were horses of various colours, red, black, piebald and white' (Zech. vi). The night here spoken of meaneth this world as it was before the coming of the Son. As ISAIAH saith, 'In the night-time my soul taketh refuge with Thee' (Isaiah xxvi. 9).

The [red] horse [with the rider on him] is ADAM, whom CHRIST dressed. And the man [on the horse] of whom he speaketh is CHRIST who put on the Virgin MARY. And he stood between two mountains, that is to say he stood between the New Law and the Old Law. And behind him there were red horses which mean the Apostles, that is to say, those who are red with the blood of their martyrdoms. And the black horses of which he speaketh are those who were in the days of the Apostles, those wicked men who came and whom people call ARIUS and NESTORIUS. And the piebald [Fol. 57*a*, col. 2] horses of which he speaketh are the Christians whose Faith was not pure [*or*, refined], and whom men call LEYÔ and

Explanations by St. John

NESṬERÔS and 'AWṬAKÎYÔS (EUTYCHIANS), and MAḴDÔNYÔS (MACE-
DONIANS), and SABÂLYÔS (SIBELLIANS), and many others who are like
unto them. And the white horses of which he speaketh are the Three
Hundred and Eighteen Orthodox Fathers, whose Faith was bright
and shining, and whose doctrine was more brilliant than the sun.

And JOHN saith: the angel who came first told me, saying:—And
when the sixth blew his trumpet, and when one-half of the sixth
period(?) [had expired] the prophets prophesied, and they sowed
seed, and others reaped, even as ISAIAH saith, 'Six sowed, three
came.' And the three who reaped were the Apostles; they were the
[Fol. 57b, col. 1] reapers, for they reaped what the Prophets had
sown. And the six who sowed, of whom he speaketh, are the Five
[Books] of the 'ÔRÎT of MOSES, and the Six Books of the Prophets.
And concerning [this] our Lord saith, 'One soweth and another
reapeth' (John iv. 57). And again ISAIAH saith, 'The ox shall not
have dominion over the yoke, nor the pot he who maketh [the pot].'
This hath reference to the 'ÔRÎT and the Prophets. There are none
who have dominion [over the 'ÔRÎT], and there is no one who can
make the pot (i.e. the Prophets). The which saith JOHN the Baptist
whose side was not pierced for the deliverance of ADAM and his
children. And ṣaheb is the name of seḵuerat, and in like manner
seḵuerat is the same as ṣaheb. Hearken thou to SÎRÂK who saith,
'Heed the fool as much as thou wouldst a broken pot.'

And at the sixth period was heard a voice from the [Fol. 57b,
col. 2] horns of the altar which said, 'The one word which is
uttered is the Only Son; His Word is to the Father, and His Word
is to the Holy Spirit. And the [four] horns are the four archbishops,
one of EPHESUS, one of ANTIOCH, one of ALEXANDRIA, and one of
ROME, which is the great throne of PETER.

And the sixth angel of whom he speaketh is the Son, and the
Four Angels of whom he speaketh are the Four Evangelists.

115

Explanations by St. John

The river EUPHRATES of which he speaketh is the Holy Church.

And the horses of which he speaketh are the thousands of Christians.

And the helmets of fire of which he speaketh are the Faith of the Father, and the Son, and the Holy Ghost.

And the heads of the horses which he saith are like unto the heads of lions, are the chiefs of the Christians and the Apostles . . . . [Fol. 58a, col. 1].

And the fire which went forth from their mouths, as he saith, are the tongues of fire which went forth from the Apostles [at Pentecost]. And the three-quarters of the children of men of which he speaketh are the three-quarters of the people in the world who have died, and who rejected the Faith at the preaching of the Apostles. The Prophets and the Apostles are called 'lions', and the Only One is also called a lion, and SATAN also is compared to a lion.

We must not in any way compare SATAN to our Lord, yet with all his mighty powers SATAN is to be compared to the lion. The Apostle saith, 'Your enemy is the Devil (GÂNÊN), who roareth like a lion and seeketh prey to devour' (1 Peter v. 8). So our Saviour calleth him a lion. Hear what the Book of [Fol. 58a, col. 2] JOB saith, 'The lion roareth and the young lions growl.' And the roaring of which he speaketh is ''ÊLÔHÊ, 'ÊLÔHÊ' on the wood of the Cross (Matt. xxvii. 40; Mark xv. 34). And the whelps are the Holy Church, which crieth out, saying, 'In the blood of His side He baptized me.' And JACOB saith, 'Thou shalt lie down there and shall rise up like a lion there being none who shall disturb thee' (Num. xxiv. 9). And when thou hast heard the prophecy of JACOB, thou shalt not imagine that it concerneth JUDAH his son, but that he prophesied about the Son. And as they called the prophets lions, so NAHUM the prophet saith, 'Where are the dens of the lions, and where are the whelps of the lions to be seen?' (Nahum ii. 12). And when he saith, 'Where are

116

the dens of the lions,' he maketh reference to [Fol. 58*b*, col. 1] those who have gone down into SHEOL, viz. the early Fathers and the Prophets. And when he saith, 'Where are the whelps of the lions to be seen?' he maketh reference to the sons of the Prophets. And when he saith, 'Where hath the Lion gone?' he meaneth CHRIST who went down into SHEOL. As BARTHOLOMEW said, 'Whither didst Thou go when thou didst descend from Thy Cross?' And our Lord JESUS said unto Him, 'Straightway I went down into SHEOL so that I might deliver the Fathers.' And NAHUM the prophet saith openly, 'Come hither, O whelps of the Lion.' And again he saith, 'He filled His side with that which He hunted(?)', which is to say, when He was hunting SATAN He filled His side with His generous blood. And when the KHARÂWÎ speared Him blood and water oozed forth [Fol. 58*b*, col. 2], and forthwith we were sealed [as] believers. And by the strengthening of the Faith those who treasured the Faith were sealed, and every one who had His Faith in him became strong. And there was no doubt, and he had no confidence in the bow of the devils. And his country was girt about with a knotted cord which could not be untied, and there was one who held in restraint the inhabitant thereof, that is to say, He bound together and baptized the Holy Church by the water which poured from His great side.

And the Evangelists have called them 'horns,' even as ZECHARIAH saith, 'I saw four openings which set free the horns, and these are the Four Archbishops who proclaimed (*or*, declared) the Gospels.' And concerning this JOHN saith, 'A voice was heard from the horns of the altar [Fol. 59*a*, col. 1] saying, The Holy Church.'

And when the angel had said all these things unto me, I said unto our father JOHN, 'Tell me the interpretation of thy words.' And he said unto me, 'About what art thou asking?' And I said, '[I am asking] about the beast (*or*, serpent), one of the heads of which was speared, and about the word which was uttered, and his death wound [which] liveth.' And the Apostle said, 'The beast (*or*, serpent) of which he speaketh is SATAN, one of whose heads was speared, and he showeth [thereby] that the kingdom of SATAN was speared by the Cross of JESUS CHRIST, and the death of all the work of SATAN who reigned in the world before the coming of the Son. And the Son came and [SATAN'S Kingdom] was destroyed by the death of CHRIST. And his death wound [Fol. 59*a*, col. 2] which liveth, concerning which the Apostle speaketh is the kingdom of the False CHRIST which came into being by the will of SATAN.

[THE NUMBER OF THE BEAST]

And the number of that Beast was $600 + 60 + 6$, and it is as great as that of the children of men. When he saith that it is 'as great as that of the children of men' he meaneth that ADAM came in his stead, even as the prophet saith in the country of SEʿÛR, for there he dwelt. And the $600 + 60 + 6$ which he gives are the names of SATAN, $A = 200$, $S = 300$ (*sic*), $M = 200$, $YÂBÊ = 30$, $DÎ = 30 + 6$. And these are the names of the captains of the army of SATAN, A meaneth Devils, S meaneth SATAN, M meaneth MÂSTÊMÂ, YÂ meaneth YÂYA, BÊ meaneth BÊLHOR, DÎ meaneth DÎABOLUS.[1]

And moreover the Book of Revelation saith: 'Another angel came (Rev. xvii. 1?), and he was carrying [Fol. 59*b*, col. 1] the Evangelist', that is to say JOHN the Baptist. And he telleth thee plainly that he giveth forgiveness, and preacheth, and saith, 'The hour of judgement hath come', that is 'the kingdom of heaven hath drawn nigh'.

And [there was] another angel (Rev. xviii. 2) who said, 'BABYLON hath fallen'. Now he was the Son who said 'the world hath fallen'.

And the third angel of whom he speaketh is PETER the Apostle.

[1] On these numbers see above, p. 97.

The Seven Vials

The words, 'Blessed are those who have died for the sake of the Word of God' refer to the Apostles.

'And I saw a sheet of glass which was like unto the sea, and it was surrounded (*or*, mingled) with fire.' The glass of which he speaketh symbolizeth the saints, and the sea of which he speaketh is the Church. And those who have conquered the Beast and [Fol. 59*b*, col. 2] stand on the sea of which he speaketh are those who believe and have been baptized.

[THE SEVEN VIALS]

And I will also speak of the Seven Vials. The Seven Vials of which he speaketh are the Seven Prophets who have risen up in their various times, and they are girded about with belts of gold. The gold of which he speaketh is the Faith. And the Seven Vials of which he speaketh are seven angels, and when he saith the 'first vial' he meaneth the first angel, and angel hath the same meaning as envoy (*or*, messenger). The first angel is MOSES, the chief of the Prophets, who poured out the wrath of God in EGYPT. And the 'ôrît (Pentateuch) telleth thee plainly how MOSES, this hater of evil, attacked those men, and punished them with enmity when he sprinkled the ashes of [Fol. 60*a*, col. 1] the furnace over them.

And another angel poured his vial into the sea. Now the angel of whom he speaketh here was JOSHUA, the son of NUN. And the sea turned into blood, and every living thing which was therein died. The sea is the world, and the blood of which he speaketh is the slaughter (*or*, battle) which took place in the days of JOSHUA. And the death of all of them of which he speaketh hath reference to the utter destruction of the CANAANITES, for they spared no one except the men of GIBEON who were crafty and pretended to be men from a remote country. And in JERICHO they spared RAHAB. Now JOSHUA is to be interpreted as the 'ôrît (Pentateuch) and the prophets who were expecting the coming of our Lord, and RAHAB is to be interpreted as the Church of the Gentiles. And the whore [Fol. 60*a*, col. 2], as he calleth her, hath reference to the whoredoms of the Gentiles. And as to the red mark which RAHAB tied to the window of her house, that symbolizeth the red blood which poured down from the side [of our Lord] on the day of Friday, at the spearing of the Beloved One.

The twelve stones which JOSHUA chose when he crossed to JORDAN are to be interpreted by the Twelve Apostles. And the one day became the second day of which he speaketh; so likewise was it at the crucifixion of our Lord, which was the day of Friday; it became two days. The day of MOSES is to be interpreted as the day of the Father. Now thou must not imagine, O man, that the Father, and the Son, and the Holy Ghost have different days. For the Father, and the Son, and the Holy Spirit are equal [Fol. 60*b*, col. 1], and one doth not precede the other, neither doth one come behind the other.

And the third angel who poured out his vial is to be interpreted as SAMUEL the prophet. The rivers and streams and fountains of water of which he speaketh are the House of ISRAEL. The blood of which he speaketh is the sacrifices of the 'ÔRÎT; and the streams of water is the cleaving of the water of the 'ÔRÎT. And the angel of the cleaving of the water of whom he speaketh is 'ÊLÎ the priest. And when he saith, 'They poured out the blood of Thy prophets', he meaneth the blood from the altar which the prophets sprinkled. And the sons of ÊLÎ, HOPHNI and PHINEHAS, defiled the altar, and the law for the offering of sacrifice was forsaken by them and they shed the blood without sprinkling it [Fol. 60*b*, col. 2], and the blood of the sacrifice. And because they shed the blood and did not sprinkle it, their own blood was shed instead of it, and was fixed(?) in their mouths. And concerning this the Book saith, 'And their blood was . . . for them after the manner(?) which was meet for them.' This is what he (i.e. the angel) told me, and it is a saying of a secret mystery. No one among men can explain it and expound(?) his word.

When he saith, 'And the fourth angel poured out his vial unto the sun', the sun which is spoken of is ELIJAH the prophet, because he laid fetters on the heavens. And he telleth thee plainly that there was burning heat and blazing fire, and men were burnt up thereby. The fire of which he speaketh was hunger, for to the belly hunger is fire. And men blasphemed (*or*, cursed) [Fol. 61*a*, col. 1] God, and the house of 'AKÂ'B denied [the existence] of the Creator.

And the fifth angel poured out his vial. And above his habitation, the habitation of which he speaketh,[1] and he who poured out the vial was the speaker of prophecy, that is ISAIAH, the son of AMÔS. And the Beast was MENASSEH, who triumphed over ISAIAH. And his words 'his Kingdom became dark' mean that he went to the country of BABYLON a captive.

And the sixth angel poured out his vial into the river EUPHRATES. The river EUPHRATES spoken of here is the House of ISRAEL. And the power out of the vial was EZEKIEL. The drying up of its waters of which he speaketh has reference to the water of the voice (*or*, word) of God, who brought to an end in ISRAEL, as was proper, the roads of the kings [Fol. 61*a*, col. 2] from the eastern quarter of the sun. The kings here spoken of are the kings of PERSIA.

And the seventh angel poured out his vial into the winds; now the angel was JOHN the Baptist, and the words of which he speaketh are the multitude of nations. And he speaketh of the drying up of the water because JOHN the Baptist, the last of the prophets, had come to an end, and because JOHN was the crown of the prophets. And similarly in seven stages the world shall be destroyed.

---

[1] Some words omitted(?).

Clement's King List

'Tell me,' I said unto the Apostle ['who these are']. And he said unto me.

'AZATABḤĔL 'ESÊWÔS is he who killed JAMES, brother of our Lord JESUS, and behold it is he who is called 'ARÔN [Fol. 61b, col. 1] the second.

And he who is called Ṭ is TIBERIUS the Second, the son of TIBERIUS the First.

And he who is called ḲA is ḲARÎNÔS the king of NINEVEH.

And he who is called KA is KABÎR, the king of PERSIA.

And he who is called SE is SEGAR, the son of 'ATÔR, king of NE'MÂR of the children of ESAU.

And he who is called A is 'ALYÂNÔS, the governor [who slew] MERCURIUS(?) the martyr.

And he who is called MA is MAXIMIANUS.

And he who is called A is AGRIPPA, who is DIOCLETIAN.

And he who is called M is MÊGÊLNES, the king of ANTIOCH.

And he who is called 'A is 'AṬÂ(?), the great king of ROME.

And he who is called ḲA is ḲARÎBÎN, the king of KUERGÎ, and he was of the seed [Fol. 61b, col. 2] of JAPHET. And when he rose up to wage war at seed-time, he perished during a difficult (or, cruel) harvest. And this saying is a wonderful thing.

The ḲUE of which he speaketh is CONSTANTINUS [the First], and the Ḳ of whom he speaketh is CONSTANTINE the Second.

The Five Kings of whom he speaketh. Their names are these: 'ARÂ, SA'Ê, WALA, LAWEN [and] PARA'ĔYA. And he speaketh of WÂ, that is WÂRGESHZAYM. . . . And again when he speaketh of WÂ that is WÂGIR, the king of PERSIA.

The YÂ of whom he speaketh is YÂ'ÊL, the king of ROME, who was of the children of ESAU. And this one became orthodox(?).

MÂ of whom he speaketh is MÂMÂE, and he was of the seed of JAPHET.

The LA of whom he speaketh is LEBÊNÎ who became orthodox(?).

RAKHA, of whom he speaketh is RAKHAMÂN, who is 'ALÂWÎ.

Ṭ of whom he speaketh is ṬÎBÔR [Fol. 62a, col. 1].

H of whom he speaketh is HERḲÂS.

M of whom he speaketh is MARCIANUS, in whose days the Cross was missing (*or*, stolen), and he came into the sea carrying it.

[THE FALSE CHRIST]

And again he saith unto thee: 'There shall be raised up the king of TÊMÂN who shall be like unto an ox, who is the False CHRIST who shall be a similitude of CHRIST. He shall be raised up saying, 'I am CHRIST.' The whelp of the lion of which he speaketh is the king of ROME. And he shall be with the king of ETHIOPIA and shall make a bond [with him], and forthwith there shall be a season of prosperity. And straightway food shall be abundant (*or*, increase), and honey, and oil, and the milk of animals. And a man shall weep in the graves [Fol. 62a, col. 2] of his neighbours, one by one. And so and so shall say, 'Rise up and come here, for food is abundant, and honey, and oil'. And a small quantity of seed soon shall become much food. And the apparel wherewith a man covereth himself shall last for a period of seven years. Now to all these things which I have told thee [give] thy mind, and this speech is a mystery.

[THE SCRIPTURES OF THE NEW LAW]

Now hearken unto me so that I may tell thee about the Books which are hidden in the New Law. Four are in the Holy Gospel, as the Book sayeth. And there are in it others which our Lord JESUS composed, many which are not written in this book. And in PETER he saith Twelve, even as he himself sayeth, but of these [Fol. 62*b*, col. 1] only a very few are revealed unto us. And of PAUL Four, even as he himself sayeth, and I have heard of a discourse(?) about what shall not happen to a man. And of JOHN Seven, according to that discourse. And the words Seven Orders must be interpreted by 'the voice of Seven Earthquakes', even as we have said before. And of JAMES One. And behold all these Books are Twenty-eight. And this word is given to man as a mystery, even as our Lord saith, 'The mysteries which appertain to Me are given to those who are followers of Me.' And this Book shall not be revealed to every man whom thou shalt meet, but only to those who are learned and to men of understanding.

Now the sons of MOSES the prophet preserved a little book (*or*, a few works) which their father had left to them and to their children's children [Fol. 62*b*, col. 2]. And when they revealed that book to all men, an angel came, and seized it, and carried it up into heaven. Now, I have related unto thee these many words of mystery: keep them carefully and reveal not [to any man] how thou hast acquired them.

And when the angel had said all these things the Apostle went up [into heaven], and the angel who remained taught me all these mysteries. And he said unto me, 'Thy peace. . . .' And then I wept copiously. And that angel said unto me, 'Weep not, for no being of flesh hath seen thy habitation.' And as concerning the Word of God for which thou hast sought much, that shall be thy fruit in the heavens. For the light of the body is the eye [Fol. 63*a*, col. 1], and the light of the soul is the Word of God. And having heard this he rejoiced and made a great feast, and there rejoiced with him four thousand times ten thousand children.

The Seasons for reading this Book appointed

Blessed shall be the man who shall cause this book to be read and who shall recite it. And he shall be saved in the Trial (i.e. Judgement), and shall not be destroyed, and he shall receive his wages in the heavens. And this book shall be read from the second day of the week of the Passion, and a man shall read it as often as he can on the eighth day, and on the festival of JOHN who saw this mystery, and on the festival of Mount TÂBÔR, and on the festival of MICHAEL of ḤEDÂR, and on the festival of the . . . of the Four Beasts. And to those who wish to make a copy of this book he saith, It is only to be found in the country (or, district) of . . . , which . . . and also in [Fol. 63a, col. 2] DENKUANÂ. And they shall commemorate Abbâ BAṢALÔTA MÎKÂ'ÊL on the seventh day of KHADÂR. May his prayer be with us, Amen.

Praise and glory are meet for the Trinity.

Amen and Amen.

PART III

[FIRST. A DISSERTATION ON THE MYSTERY OF THE GODHEAD]

The Father doth not precede the Son.

And the Son doth not precede His Father.

And the Holy Spirit doth not precede the Father.

And the Son is One.

They existed before the world was created;

And One was their existence after the creation of the world.

There was never a time when they were not in being.

And it can never happen that they are not in being.

It is impossible to say concerning them 'Then did they at such and such a time thus come into being, and they will endure until such and such [a time].

126

A Hymn of Praise to the Sea of Mercy

There was no beginning to their existence, and there will be no end to their existence.

They are One [in] Three and Three [in] One.

[A HYMN OF PRAISE TO GOD]

Praise be [Fol. 63*b*, col. 1] unto Him, the Lover of men, O Thou sea of mercy and humility!

Companion of men of sin, and Companion of the God of mercy.

Companion of men who have transgressed, and Companion of the God of mercy and forgiveness of transgressions.

He bestoweth honour on the man with whom He is pleased, and He abaseth in the dust the man whom He will abase.

He exalteth whom He pleaseth, and He humbleth whom He pleaseth.

He leaveth to men [who are His pleasure] portions of [His] possessions; some He promoteth to honour, and some He reduceth [to beggary].

To some He apportioneth a measure of honey and oil, and some who are in it He maketh to be beaten with fire, and wood, and stone.

Some He magnifieth, and some He sanctifieth, and some He reduceth to poverty.

Blessed be the name of the words of His chariot, and His tabernacle [Fol. 63*b*, col. 2] of fire, and His tents.

He hath made a similitude of water in His apparel, and the clouds are the dust of His feet, and the water of the sea cannot hold (i.e. contain) His fist.

He hath bound the sea with cords, and the extent thereof is a journey of one thousand years; and it shall be called the resting-place of His feet. And moreover, on the top of His place of movement is the expanse of the cold sea.

With His Father and with the Holy Spirit, hidden(?) dwelleth the Son with His Father and with the Holy Spirit, and they praise Him (i.e. the Father) in His awful tabernacle. Their horses are fashioned of flames of fire, and their motion is terrifying. And when they hear a little word of the Creator they tremble and are dismayed (*or*, sorely frightened). And [Fol. 64*a*, col. 1] the Creator saith unto them, 'Be not afraid, and be not frightened; carry ye me even as I carry you.' And with great joy, when they wish to travel, the chariot is lifted up with them, and He arriveth with them on the earth or is lifted up into the heavens. There is no contention (*or*, strife) among them, and they know not how to quarrel and to disobey(?) And their hearts are opened out wide in mercy, like their God. And their censers petition for mercy, and their crosses beg for mercy, and their altars entreat for mercy, and their tabernacles ask for mercy. And their censers are the prayers of the saints, and when they offer up incense they say, 'Praise' (*or*, Glory). Fire is a [Fol. 64*a*, col. 2] vivifier of those who believe on His Name, and it is a punishment to those who do not believe on Him. And that fire goeth forth from a bosom of fire, and the sea honoureth(?).

And the Third One is not less than the Two of them, and as concerning the power of the Third One, hearken and I will tell thee. The Father said, 'Let us make man in our image and likeness.' And the Son said, 'I will put on the flesh of ADAM.' And the Holy Spirit said, 'I will dwell in the hearts of the Prophets and Apostles, and in the hearts of all the saints who believe on Me with integrity of heart and with purity of mind.' And the Godhead is with the Incarnation, One Being. The Father did not abandon the being of the Father, and the Son did not abandon the being of the Son, nor the Holy Spirit the being of the Holy Spirit [Fol. 64*b*, col. 1], but was equal with them.

The Father was He who sent, the Son was He who was sent, and the Holy Spirit was well pleased with the work.

Christ the First and the Last

The Father was He who begot, and not He who was begotten; the Son was He who was begotten, and not He who begot; and the Holy Spirit was well pleased with their plan. They were those who had power to take, and there was none who could take (i.e. contain) them. They were dominators and there was none who could dominate them. He knew man without having created him, and there was none who possessed the power of knowing them accurately, for they had power to slay, and there was none who was able to slay them. Who knew when to kill him and when to give him life?

And after this speech the shining being answered and said unto my father BAKHAYLA MÎKÂ'ÊL, 'Hearken and I will tell thee a mystery, the explanation of the creation of the heavens and the earth. The work which was done [Fol. 64b, col. 2] on the first day was the symbol of [that done] on the last day, at the coming of the Lord. The first day was a symbol of the day of His new Resurrection on the first day. The things which were created were symbols of the establishments of the Church. Observe that in the 'ÔRÎT the Trinity speaketh and saith, 'In the beginning God made the heavens.' The beginning of which he speaketh was CHRIST, even as ISAIAH the prophet saith, 'I am the first and I am the last.' And JOHN saith that He was the first, and PAUL saith that CHRIST was the first. And again, JOHN the Evangelist saith unto thee, 'The Word was the first.' And MARK the Evangelist saith, [Fol. 65a, col. 1] 'The first of the Gospel(?) is JESUS CHRIST, the son of God.'

And concerning the Holy Spirit the 'ÔRÎT speaketh to thee openly and saith that it 'hovered over the water'. Observe then that the Trinity is mentioned openly at the beginning of the 'ÔRÎT. In that he saith that the earth existed at an earlier time he maketh allusion to the Church which existed aforetime in the heart of God. The darkness over the water of which he speaketh symbolizeth the darkness of the synagogue of the JEWS. And 'the deep' is a symbol of the 'ôRîT. And 'heaven' is the symbol of the Apostles, even as they themselves [Fol. 65a, col. 2] say, 'Make for us our mouth as wide as the heavens, we pray.' And the fire is the symbol of life-giving fire. And the water is the symbol of baptism. And the wind (*or*, air) is the symbol of the Holy Spirit. And the Holy Spirit is the first (i.e. oldest) of all creation. And the holy angels are symbols of the priests. And 'let there be light' which He commanded at the beginning, is the symbol of that word which He spake, 'He who hath believed and is baptized shall be saved.'

Everything which took place at the beginning is a symbol of the last day. The 'ôRîT is a symbol of the Gospel, and the Gospel is a symbol of that Voice which calleth to the righteous, saying, 'Come to Me, ye blessed of My Father [Fol. 65b, col. 1], that ye may inherit My kingdom which is prepared for you.' The words 'he who believeth not shall be condemned', are a symbol of that Voice [which saith], 'Depart ye, O cursed ones to that which is prepared for SATAN and his angels.'

And the Tabernacle of ISRAEL is the shadow of the Church, and the Church is the shadow of JERUSALEM which is in the heavens.

The 'ôRîT is the shadow of the Holy Gospel, and the Holy Gospel is the shadow of the New World.

The Prophets are shadows of the Apostles, and the Apostles are the shadows of those who live the life of the angels.

The priests of the 'ôRîT are the shadows of the priests of the Gospel, and the priests of the Gospel are the shadows of the priests of heaven. But the priests of the Gospel have far greater authority than the priests of heaven. The latter cannot grasp the mystery [Fol. 65b, col. 2] without the tongs of fire, but the priests of the Gospel hold it in their hands. And for this reason God said, 'ADAM hath become like one of us. Peradventure he will lift up his hand and eat of the Tree of Life and live for ever like one of us.' He saith, 'one of us', and here 'one' means the Son. 'Peradventure he will lift up his hand' hath reference to the priests who lift up their hands to eat the Body of the Son. Assuredly the Tree of Life is CHRIST Himself, even as He Himself saith, 'I am the Tree of Life.' A hidden mystery dwelleth in the heart of man, that is the Faith of the Father, and the Son, and the Holy Spirit.

Here endeth the explanation of what was created on the First Day, the Sabbath [Fol. 66*a*, col. 1].

And in the second day there is the symbol of the ascent of our Lord into heaven. As the water rose up on the second day so our Lord, the water of life, went up into the heavens. As to the fourth day the water is to be interpreted in many ways. Sometimes it must be interpreted as the nations (Gentiles), and sometimes as the Church. And behold, here endeth the discourse on the mystery of the second day.

And the third day is a symbol of the fifty day[s] (i.e. Pentecost), for this symbolizes the Trinity. And on the third day God said, 'Let the waters be gathered together in one [place]', which is to say, 'Let the nations be gathered together to Him in one Faith.' And the dry land is the strong Faith. The trees are symbols of the Apostles, and must be so interpreted. And [Fol. 66*a*, col. 2] the green herbs are the symbols of the children of the Apostles, and the children of the Apostles are those who have believed through their hands. And the seed are those servants who have sown seed on the face of the earth. The words 'each kind of seed' refer to their various companies, and to their various preachings. The Garden is to be interpreted as the Church, and the flowers and flowering shrubs of the Garden are to be interpreted as the Christian people. And as for the seed of various kinds and forms and species: The first kind belong to the God of Israel, and are those who have believed in Him, and the Christians who have believed on Him; these are the kin of God. And again the seed is the Word of God. And in that he saith, 'It shall be food for the birds of heaven,' birds [Fol. 66*b*, col. 1] must be interpreted as the angels of heaven. And these are they who have believed firmly in the Word of God which is preached under the heavens, and who say, 'Praise be unto Him who hath shown Himself pleased with men.'

The four rivers are to be interpreted by the Four Evangelists. The first river is 'ÊPHÊSÔN. And here there is green gold, and precious stones of *yaḥtu* (jacinth?). And here there is red gold. Now thus [runs] the explanation which Abbâ BAKHAYLA MÎKÂ'ÊL told me his son ISAAC, and I have written it down that it may become the knowledge of posterity. The first river is a symbol of the country of the Gospel which MATTHEW wrote. And the green gold is the human flesh which our Lord took from MARY, even as MOSES the prophet saith [Fol. 66*b*, col. 2]: 'I saw a green bush and fire moving about in it', which is the divinity of our Lord. In this place there is precious stone, that is to say baptism. And on that day of baptism the name of a man shall come on a pillar of gold, and that name shall be a part of the portion of an angel. And that writing shall be in the portion of the angel whom he joineth on the day of baptism. And when he beginneth a fast, the angel shall join him in the fast on the sixth day and the fourth day. And when mercy is to be shown the angel of mercy joineth himself with him, and bringeth him to the angel of life, who is JESUS CHRIST the Only Son, and He saith to His Father, 'Be merciful for My sake to My people who are sealed with the blood of My side', and [Fol. 67*a*, col. 1] verily He will be merciful to him.

And as to what goeth forth from the river, the explanation thereof is that it is a symbol of the children whom HEROD slew, and verily these were dipped in the blood of martyrdom.

And the second river GEYÔN mentioned by him is a symbol of the second country of the Gospel which MARK wrote in a place on the borders of EGYPT and ETHIOPIA.

And the third river mentioned by him, the TIGRIS, is a symbol of the country of the Gospel which LUKE wrote, and it bordereth on the country of FÂRES, which is this world. And FÂRES also meaneth fire, even as ISAIAH saith, 'And He shall make might to burn(?) in FÂRES.'

And the fourth river, the EUPHRATES which bordereth YÔRDÂNÔS, is the symbol of the country of the Gospel which JOHN [Fol. 67*a*, col. 2], who was the announcer of the Deity, wrote. And JOHN wrote in the language of RÔMÊ (GREEK) to the men of EPHESUS, for EPHESUS was Greek. And LUKE wrote in the language of RÔMÊ, and MARK in ḲEBṬÎ (COPTIC) and MATTHEW in HEBREW.

And 'ÎFÊSÂN flowed with milk, which is the doctrine of JESUS CHRIST our Lord. And GEYÔN flowed with wine, that is to say the joy of His Resurrection. And the TIGRIS flowed with honey which is the symbol of His patient endurance and Passion. And the EUPHRATES flowed with oil which is the symbol of the conquest of the Godhead. This river is the inheritance of the righteous (*or*, justified) and the children. And those who have in them the law concerning transgression shall drink of the river of milk. And those who have in them the power to carry the word [Fol. 67*b*, col. 1] shall drink of the river of honey. And those who have in them the joy of the Spirit shall drink of the river of wine. And those who have devoted themselves to service of their own accord shall drink of the river of oil. All this we have mentioned because of the work which was done on the third day. Here endeth the whole discourse on the third day, and the explanation of the mystery thereof.

And on the fourth day [God] said, "Let the sun, and moon, and stars come into being!' The fourth day is a symbol of Mount TABOR. And the moon is a symbol of PETER and of all his brethren the

Apostles, and the stars are symbols of all the righteous. And that
we have compared this day to the day of Mount TABOR and made it
a symbol thereof is because of the beauty of the sun, and moon, and
stars. And the righteous of Mount TABOR are twice [as bright as] the
sun. This is the [Fol. 67*b*, col. 2] explanatory discourse concerning
the fourth day.

And [God] said on the fifth day, 'Let the waters produce fish, and
feathered fowl, and whales. And some call [the whales] BÊḤÊMÔT
and LÊWEYÂTÂN (BEHEMOTH and LEVIATHAN). Now the fifth day is to
be interpreted by the prayer of the fifth day, wherein our Lord made
manifest the taking of His flesh and blood. And the birds which
went forth on the fifth day are to be interpreted by the Apostles to
whom He gave His flesh on the evening of the fifth day. And the
fish are to be interpreted by the holy Fathers who were in SHEOL, and
who went forth through the blood of His side. And the whales[1] are
symbols of SATAN and the synagogue of the JEWS, and the . . .
symbolizes the banquet of the saints. This is the discourse about
and this is the explanation of [the work of] the fifth day.

Concerning what happened on the Eve of the Sabbath (Friday).
On Friday wild beasts, and cattle, and the '*A'mâg*, that is to say, the
reptiles [Fol. 68*a*, col. 1] were created.

And ADAM was created after all the beasts. This then is to be
interpreted as the high priests and the synagogue of the JEWS who
were gathered together in JERUSALEM on the day of Friday. And
the beasts are to be interpreted by the nations (Gentiles), for He
chose them on the Cross, and in this wise the Gentiles are called
beasts. Doth not ISAIAH speak concerning the beasts of the desert
meaning the Gentiles. And MICAH saith that the beasts are among
the beasts of the desert? And this meaneth that CHRIST is among
the Gentiles. And EZRA saith, 'A lion shall rise up out of the desert.'

[1] In the text 'panthers'!

The Creation of Adam

And as they are called beasts even so the synagogue of the JEWS is to be called beasts. Hear what JOHN the Baptist saith, 'A beast of the earth shall be born.' Who? Understand ye [Fol. 68a, col. 2]. And the prophets say, 'The beasts of the earth who shall lick the dust', which is to say, 'The rebellion which they made [against] the Creator.' Those who are beasts whom he mentions are those who have made beasts of the people who were created above ADAM and who dwell in the earth. Even as DAVID saith, 'There is the great sea here which is full of beasts without number.' The sea is the world, and those who are beasts therein are the peoples.

And for what reason was ADAM created after everything else? As ADAM was created on the Friday in like manner our Lord went up on the Cross on the day of Friday. And he saith, 'They shall all be one.' Then ADAM being created on the Friday was a symbol of the crucifixion of the Lord. And from Him the nations germinated [Fol. 68b, col. 1] when He prayed on the Cross, saying, 'They shall all be one.'

Now ADAM was created from four natural materials and the divinity of CHRIST was likewise fourfold. The day Friday is then a symbol of the crucifixion of the Lord. And on that day when blood and water flowed down from the side of that doer of beautiful deeds, the rock was split open, and that water of life entered into the mouth of ADAM and became his life. And when the spirit of the Lord JESUS went forth it descended into SHEOL, with the soul of the flesh and divinity. And His Body remained on the Cross, and the divinity was not separated again from that Body. With the soul of the flesh and with His divinity He brought out His chosen ones, and sent them so that they might enter the Garden (Paradise). And He said unto them, 'Go ye into the Garden and [Fol. 68b, col. 2] the thief who was on My right hand shall be your leader.' And when those who were justified heard this they said, 'Who is this thief on the right hand?' Is it ADAM, father of the world, or NOAH, or ABRAHAM, the friend of God, or ISAAC the pure, or JACOB the holy one, or MOSES the meek, or DAVID the remitter of sins, or SAMUEL the fourth, or SOLOMON the wise man, or JOSIAH who ruled righteously, or HEZEKIAH who walked before him in righteousness and integrity, or EZEKIEL who saw among the beasts four fires(?)? Who is this who marcheth before God and goeth joyfully? Who is this of whom our Lord sayeth, 'the thief who is on the right hand shall be your leader'? [Fol. 69a, col. 1].

And the thief answered and said unto them, 'I am not any one of those whom ye mention, but I am a man who from my youth up have washed myself in the blood of men, but kindness hath directed me, and from my youth up mercy hath been set in my heart. And [when] I have killed a man I have wept over his head, and lamented him. And it is that which hath brought me to this mercy.' And thus saying he flew upwards with joy, and in his hand he held a writing which said, 'Open ye the gates O SERÂPHÎM and CHERÛBHÎM, open ye to us, open ye to us.' And all the righteous said the same thing. And the SERÂPHÎM said, 'We will not open unto you,' and the CHERÛBHÎM said, 'We will not open unto you.' And straightway this thief who is DÊMÂS showed the CHERÛBHÎM the writing which was in his hand, and was written in the blood of the first born [Fol. 69a, col. 2] which is the blood of our Lord JESUS CHRIST, the Only Son of the Father. And when that angel read the writing, he cast away the spear of fire which was in his hand. And then there came in first of all the thief of the right hand, and closely following him came all the righteous into the Garden. ADAM, father of the world, shouted. NOAH(?) beat a drum. ABRAHAM gave thanks and praise. ISAAC glorified [God]. JACOB sang praises. MOSES clapped his hands. AARON pronounced a blessing. SAMUEL rejoiced. DAVID played the psaltery beautifully. SOLOMON was smitten with wonder. And

EZEKIEL and ISAIAH rejoiced. And ISAIAH said, 'It is SEBAOTH (i.e. hosts of God) and the foundation of His counsel which is sweet.' And JOB said, 'I will continue in His patience which beareth patiently the sin of the world.' And [Fol. 69*b*, col. 1] JEREMIAH said, 'The Only Son hath come to life.' And EZEKIEL said, 'In DAVID His servant He looked upon us(?)' And DANIEL said, 'A revelation (*or*, vision) of the prophets hath become visible.' And ZECHARIAH said, 'Light hath risen up from a man.' AMOS said, 'Gladness hath spread itself abroad in all the earth.' And 'ÎYÂSU took the drum from the hand of NOAH, and sang sweetly, saying, 'Let the heavens rejoice and let the earth be glad.' And the whole company of the prophets danced, and leaped about, and cried out and said, 'Praise be unto Him, unto our Lord in [the heavens], Who [hath brought us] to this, the beginning of our inheritance, because He hath bestowed upon us life through His death.' And it was not only they who rejoiced, but all those who were in the heavens, and also those who were on the earth were glad. This is the story which we have related concerning the work which was created on the day of Friday. Glory be unto Him the Creator.

And on the first [Fol. 69*b*, col. 2] SANBAT (Sabbath) He rested in His Trinity, and He commanded that the Trinity should rest from work. And that day is the symbol of the rest of the righteous, and thereon the holy angels keep the Sabbath. And the other angels are sent into their service of the Lord God, and they are the angels of the face, the angels of consecration. Among them there is circumcision for the angels of consecration. And similarly there is circumcision for the angels of the face, and the angels of consecration. Hear how the Book of KUAFÂLÊ saith, 'Thus is the circumcision of the angels of consecration.' Therefore it is right that we all should say, 'Praise be unto Him who hath created us for everlasting life.' Amen.

God provides for Adam after His Ejection from Paradise

And ISAAC, the son of Abbâ BAṢALÔTA MÎKÂ'ÊL, saith, 'I will add a further discourse.' And he wrote the following computation of the sun [Fol. 70a, col. 1], that is to say the computation which declareth how the great TANÂBLET, that is the prophets, were born, from ADAM to CHRIST the King. According to what the Book of the Law saith, twenty-two administrations were formed from ADAM to NÊHÛ, or twenty-two generations. And according to this twenty-two heads were born from ADAM to CHRIST the King. And that thou mayest find the day of the birth of ADAM. Take the [number of] the administrations . . . and the Epact, and add thereto the four elements [which form ADAM]. Subtract each seven(?) and add one, and there will remain seven. That is the birth[day] of ADAM, the seventh day of MÎYÂZYÂ.[1]

When this first ADAM sinned he went forth [Fol. 70a, col. 2] from the Garden, and our Lord went down to save him from hard labours. ADAM went forth from his inheritance on Friday, and our Lord went forth from ḲARÂNYÔ[2] on the day of Friday to be crucified. ADAM ate [of the tree] on the third hour, and ADAM and EVE stripped(?) the tree of the Garden. And in like manner the back of our Lord was scourged with forty stripes until the blood flowed, and the punishments which our Lord bore after this were innumerable. And when ADAM went forth from the Garden our Lord gave him twelve oxen. And to EVE He gave a gift likewise. And the bees went forth with her from the Garden. And sheep, five male and five female, and goats, [Fol. 70b, col. 1] five male and five female, went forth with her. And mules went forth with her, two male and two female, and from the fornication of the two of them God multiplied children. And God also gave them shoots of the trees of the Garden, that is to say young plants which ADAM took out of the Garden. And one of them

---

[1] I do not know the system, and the correctness of the translation of this passage is very doubtful.　　　　[2] i.e. the 'place of a skull'.

was 'ÊLYÂS, that is to say the olive. And for this reason the 'ÔRÎT saith, 'the land of 'ÊLYÂS, which is the olive, 2 NARD, 3 which is NÂRGÊ, and KARKÂ 4, which is the lemon with abundant fruit. 'ÊN-GÛTÂT 5, which is ṬERNEGUE. TAMAR 6. And LAWEZ, and GAWAZ, and SEKAR. Wine and TABAL, which is HEYNESÂT.' All these did the SERÂPHÎM and CHERÛBHÎM give him by the command of the Living God. And ADAM went forth from the Garden [Fol. 70*b*, col. 2], and the angels who had charge of the trees of the Garden wept with him, and they escorted him twelve leagues. Therefore it is meet for people to escort a neighbour when he setteth out on a journey.

And as ADAM planted the young trees of the Garden, so our Lord planted on His departure the Twelve Apostles and the Seventy Disciples, and each of the Saints contended in his own way. This is the discourse wherewith we commemorate the creation of ADAM.

PART IV

The Birth of Enoch

The breastplate and its stones and their symbolism.
The descent of the Apostles from the sons of JACOB.
On Almsgiving.
Incense and prayer.
The five goats are the princes of PHILISTIA.
The five ewes are the five wise virgins.
Symbolism of the censer, and the TÂBÔT.
The TÂBÔT and MARY the Virgin.
MOSES, JOB, JOSHUA. RAHAB and the red cord.
DAVID a symbol of the Son.

AND NOW WE WILL RECORD ANOTHER DISCOURSE CONCERNING THE BIRTH OF ENOCH,[1] who was the seventh from ADAM.

From his birth he kept righteousness, and he saw (*or*, watched) everything which happened and marvelled. Moreover, he had visions concerning the sun and the moon and the stars [Fol. 71*a*, col. 1]. And all the prophets are symbols of the Son. And ENOCH wrote twelve Institutes and Sabbaths, and God the Father wrote with His finger the Ten Commandments.

And ENOCH saith, 'I was born on the first Sabbath, and I waited patiently until the coming of righteousness. This word righteousness hath reference to the Son. For at the first Sabbath there was rest, and at the birth of our Lord all creation was at rest. ENOCH saith, 'I waited until righteousness came'; and ENOCH waited until that time.

And in the second Sabbath ENOCH saw a vision of an evil and crafty camel, and by means of it he delivered a man—he saith. The man of whom he speaketh was NOAH whom he saved from the waters of the Flood [Fol. 71*a*, col. 2].

The next Sabbath of which he speaketh was his own days. And in the days of ḲÂYÂL (CAIN) and his children the Law was evil and polluted. And these boasted themselves over ADAM, that is those

---

[1] For a list of the principal works dealing with the Book of Enoch see the translation by Charles.

who were angels and who were clothed with flesh, and they taught great sin. And these made symbols of everything which they saw in the heavens, and they taught sin because of their pride and boast-fulness, because they had clothed themselves with flesh, but it was unseemly for men to boast themselves because of this. Blessed is the man who having put on flesh conquereth SATAN. Now ḲÂYÂL was the father of ENOCH. And ENOCH begot GÂYDÂD, and GÂYDÂD begot MALAL'ÊL, and MALAL'ÊL begot MÂTÛSALA. And MÂTÛSALA begot LÂMÊKH, and LÂMÊKH was the counterpart of SATAN [Fol. 71*b*, col. 1]. And LÂMÊKH killed ḲÂYÂL who was one of his children. And SATAN killed ADAM who was the seventh of the seven works which God created on the first day of the week. And ḲÂYÂL was avenged by the seventy-seven floods of rain, and ADAM was avenged by the seventy-seven tribes of the sea carrying him away. These are they whom LUKE the Evangelist mentioneth.

Now let us go back to the narrative of ENOCH. In the third Sabbath ENOCH saith, 'He chose a man for a plant of righteousness, who was ABRAHAM.'

And in the fourth Sabbath [he saith], 'He called out a man, and a tabernacle was made for them.' The man of whom he speaketh was MOSES, whom God called in HOREB. And the tabernacle which was made for them, of which ENOCH speaketh, was the tabernacle (*or*, tent) of ISRAEL which was constructed by human art.

And in the fifth Sabbath was seen the vision [Fol. 71*b*, col. 2] [which concerned] the time of the Prophets.

And in the sixth Sabbath he saith, 'And in it a man shall be made to go up, and the tribes shall disperse a root of excellence.' And the man of whom he speaketh was CHRIST who went up upon the Cross. The root of which he speaketh, which was to be dispersed, was the House of ISRAEL which was to be dispersed by His Crucifixion.

And in the seventh Sabbath to the time of which he speaketh

must be given a twofold exposition(?) of doctrine. This was the period of those who knew of the coming of the Lord. And the second doctrine whereof he speaketh is the Old and the New [Testaments]. And he saith that this generation shall [endure] a day because of the day of RÔMÊ, and the RABÂʿYÂN who talk about a god, who being a man hath become God, whereas we say, 'He was God and became [Fol. 72a, col. 1] a man, our Lord.' And His divinity was not separated from His humanity for a single hour, or even for the twinkling of an eye. ARIUS denied the humanity of the Son, saying, 'Our God was not born of a woman.' Others have adduced many different kinds of perverted views, but they have all been sealed for SHEOL.

And in the eighth Sabbath he saith, 'A sword shall be given in it.' This Sabbath is the time of the Three Hundred and Eighteen orthodox Fathers. The sword of which he speaketh is the Word of God. And in the eighth Sabbath he saith, 'There shall be built a great royal house', that is to say the Christian Churches which were built in the time of the Emperor CONSTANTINE.

And the ninth Sabbath he saith, is the period of the 'ALWÎYÂN: their friends [Fol. 72a, col. 2] and their names. . . .

And the tenth Sabbath, he saith, is the time of the False CHRIST, which is the end of the world. Then shall be fulfilled everything according to what DANIEL the prophet said, 'Then shall be the end of the world.' And all this ENOCH saw before it took place.

In order to find out where ENOCH the prophet was born, take four names of the moon, [and the names of] the seven windows of heaven, and two names of the sun, and his name, and the name of his son, and reject (or, divide?) by seven, and there will remain seven exactly. That is the day of the birth of ENOCH, on the seventh day of the month of KHADÂR. And that the day of the birth of NOAH may be found, take the name of [his father], and the name of his mother, and the names of his three children, and the name of his wife, and the names of his sons' wives, and ... [Fol. 72b, col. 1] and the Epact, and two; reject(?) by seven, and there will remain seven, which is the day of the birth of NOAH, on the seventh of MÎGÂZYÂ.[1]

And on the day when NOAH was born he uttered praises, knowing what would happen in the later time, when the children would praise with Hosannas. Now NOAH was a symbol of the Son; hearken then and I will tell thee. NOAH made a TÂBÔT, a symbol of the Christian Church. Its height,[2] 500 [cubits], of which he speaketh, was a symbol of 500 persons (?), and its width as he saith, 300 cubits, was a symbol of the Three Hundred and Eighteen orthodox Fathers. The thirty beams of which he speaketh are a symbol of the fruits of the faithful.

And the washing by the water of the Flood through the winds [and] the wrath of God, are a symbol of the baptism which blew away the soul from the worship of idols, even as the Apostles say, 'He who hath believed in the Father [Fol. 72b, col. 2], and the Son, and the Holy Spirit, is blown away from the service of idols.'

And the sheep which NOAH sacrificed is the symbol of the Son.

And NOAH who drank wine and slept is the symbol of the sleep of the Son at the time of His Passion. And that one mocked at the nakedness of NOAH is a symbol of the company of the JEWS who mocked at JESUS. Even as the Evangelist saith, 'And they made a mock of Him, and jeered at Him' (Matt. xxvii. 29). And SHEM and JAPHET who took garments and covered the nakedness of their father is a symbol of JOSEPH and NICODEMUS who buried our Lord. And the coming sober of NOAH was the symbol of the Resurrection of CHRIST, the King.

And the devouring raven, NOAH's messenger, was the symbol of

---

[1] I do not understand the system of calculation and the translation is doubtful.
[2] Gen. vi. 15 gives 300 cubits, 50 cubits, and 30 cubits in height.

JUDAS the devourer, the steward [Fol. 73*a*, col. 1], the thief of the purse, the seller of his Lord. Why, O JUDAS, didst thou steal? Didst thou imagine that thou wouldst profit thereby? Didst thou not destroy thyself?

And the first dove which NOAH sent out was a symbol of the 'ôRîT which was sent out on SINAI. And, as he saith, it found not a resting place, because the people of the 'ôRîT did not find rest in the first Law. Even as saith ZACHARIAH, 'And he who came in to me did not rest, neither did he who went forth cease from suffering', that is to say, 'He who was put to death for me, and he who was born for me, did not rest from the suffering of SHEOL.'

And the second dove who was sent out by NOAH is a symbol of the Gospel. And the olive branch which was in the beak of the dove was a symbol of the human nature of our Lord [according to] the writing which saith [Fol. 73*a*, col. 1] in the Gospel, 'Son of DAVID, Son of ABRAHAM.' This is the discourse on NOAH showing how he became a symbol of the Only Son.

A third discourse showing how ABRAHAM was born, and how thou mayest find out his birthday. Take thee the number twenty-two from the name of his father and the name of his mother. Now we say twenty-one with ABRAHAM(?) . . . and the Epact, and three, cast away by threes(?) and then will be left seven which is the day of the birthday of ABRAHAM, the seventh day of the month of ṬER, the [day of] the circumcision of our Lord.

And ABRAHAM was perfect in everything, and God tried him with ten trials and found him trustworthy in them all. And as ABRAHAM was tried with ten trials, so he became a symbol of our Lord [Fol. 73*b*, col. 1].

ABRAHAM was tried first of all by the going out from his country, and our Lord was tried by His going forth from the land of ISRAEL and His journey into the land of EGYPT.

ABRAHAM was tried by the sterility of the land, and our Lord was tried by the Devil when He went forth to fast in the desert, and also when He said, 'We have no food wherewith to feed the people.'

ABRAHAM was tried at the burial of SÂRÂ, and our Lord was tried by the lack of some one to bury Him until JOSEPH and NICODEMUS came, and swathed Him for burial and buried Him.

ABRAHAM was tried by the battle with the ten kings who had gathered together against him, and our Lord was tried by the fight with the JEWS who had gathered together against Him, that they might kill Him on the day of Friday.

ABRAHAM conquered [Fol. 73*b*, col. 2] the tribes with three hundred and eighteen men, and our Lord pursued the people and conquered SATAN by the preaching of the Three Hundred and Eighteen orthodox Fathers.

ABRAHAM was tried by the expulsion of his son ISHMAEL who was with his mother 'AGÂR, and our Lord was tried by the death of LAZARUS His friend, although He was [the Lord] who killed and made to live.

ABRAHAM was tried when one said unto him, 'Cast out the handmaiden with her son,' and it was a hard thing to our Lord when the temple was rent asunder and its children. Now the temple was rent and torn because the people crucified Him.

ABRAHAM was tried by circumcision, and our Lord was tried by the tearing of his side by the spear. Through the circumcision of ABRAHAM grace came to the Gentiles [Fol. 74*a*, col. 1] and through the piercing of the side of our Lord life came to the Gentiles.

ABRAHAM was tried by the stopping up of his wells, and our Lord was tried by the observing of His doctrine by the bitter JEWS, who wished to hide His holy Resurrection.

And ABRAHAM was also tried by the carrying off of his wife, and our Lord was tried by the carrying off of the red cloak which was on Him, and by the robbery of the tunic which was on Him. All these things which happened [to ABRAHAM] were symbolic of our Lord. This is all the discourse which concerneth ABRAHAM.

Faith was found with ABRAHAM, and it maketh itself manifest with great certainty. And ABRAHAM was baptized with baptism, even as our Lord saith in the Book of the Covenant, 'He gave to ABRAHAM the baptism [Fol. 74a, col. 1] of life [and] the right hand.' In this discourse we have recorded some few facts so that his history may be understood. He shone with light, and his light was greater than that of twelve suns. Now the monks magnify him with the saints, that is to say, the Prophets, but they do not do so in the name of the monastic life; those who magnify him are those who are perfect in patient endurance. These are PAUL and those who are like ANTHONY and MACARIUS.

Now ANTHONY was tried with twelve trials:

1. The death of his father.
2. The Hebrew woman.
3. By the devils who were like horned bulls.
4. By phantoms of soldiers of the king's army.
5. By hunger and by thirst.
6. By the terror of MASTÊMÂ, who took the form of [Fol. 74b, col. 1] a beast which uttered terrifying cries and, in the GĔĔZ language, is called *namer* (panther).
7. By the thrust(?) of a spear of a SYRIAN.
8. By the report that he had gone back into the world.
9. By the 'ankâl, which is the hour.
10. By his patient endurance of the quarrels of the monks.
11. By the wild asses (*or*, apes) which invaded his land and wasted his crop seven times in one day.
12. By the plundering of his habitations; and by pains in the head and pains in his eyes.

Isaac's Birthday. *The Ram in the Thicket*

With these twelve trials ANTHONY was tried, and he shone with light which was greater than twelve suns, and his light was twelve times brighter than that of the Prophets. And concerning this one of the saints saith, 'ABRAHAM, who is called the "Friend of God", was sorry when he saw how great was the gift of God' [to ANTHONY]: This is [Fol. 74*b*, col. 2] all the discourse about ABRAHAM, the glorious.

AGAIN A DISCOURSE ABOUT ISAAC HIS SON. In order to find the birthday of ISAAC, take the number of twenty-two [and the name of his father], and the name of his mother, and the Epact one, and *baraket* one, and cast away seven by seven three times, and ten will be left, which is the birthday of ISAAC on the tenth day of the month of SANÊ. And this is the symbol of the festival of Pentecost, and a symbol of the wheat festival of ISRAEL.

Now ISAAC is a symbol of JESUS CHRIST, and he was pure and chaste, and he knew no other woman except REBECCA his wife. And for this reason he was given a length of days greater than those of his father. Many were his days [Fol. 75*a*, col. 1].

[THE RAM WHICH TOOK THE PLACE OF ISAAC]

A ram of Paradise was sacrificed instead of him. It was akin to the ram which ABEL sacrificed, and to the ram which ISRAEL sacrificed. It was akin to the rams which were created in the land of 'ÊLDÂ. And a portion came to JAPHET and to HAM. And the rams of Paradise came to the portion of SHEM, and how some of these rams came as a portion to SHEM, hearken and I will tell thee. For blessed is he, and blessed is he who is born from his house; and how some were born of the house of JACOB hearken and I will tell thee.

[JACOB'S BIRTHDAY]

Take the number of twenty-two fathers, the name of his father and the name of his mother, and add(?) the Epact, and seven and

148

barakat two. Cast out seven three times and there will remain eleven, which is the day of the birth of [Fol. 75*a*, col. 1] JACOB, on the eleventh day of the month of ȚER, which is the day of the baptism of our Lord. And JACOB was born on the day of ḲEDÂSÊ,[1] for he was holy, and the bearer of the pearl is glorious and blessed from the womb of his mother. And our Lord chose him and said, 'JACOB I have loved! and ESAU have I hated' (Mal. i. 3). JACOB is then a symbol of the Son, and ESAU is a symbol of SATAN. So then JACOB was blessed by his father, and ESAU was not blessed. And blessings were given to JACOB, for the Angels of the Face, and the angels of the ḲEDÂSÊ entreated, saying, 'Let blessing be upon JACOB for his heart and his mind are pure.'

When JACOB was in the tent ESAU went forth wishing to kill him [Fol. 75*b*, col. 1]. The tent which is mentioned is a symbol of the Cross and ESAU is a symbol of SATAN. And the four corners of the habitation in which JACOB was symbolize the Four Evangelists. And the going forth of the sons of JACOB to the war with ESAU is the symbol of the going forth of the Apostles to preach the Gospel. And the arrow of JACOB which killed ESAU must be interpreted by the Cross of CHRIST which killed SATAN on the day of Friday. And as JACOB gave a gift to ESAU so our Lord gave a gift and tribute to CAESAR. LABAN is to be interpreted as SATAN and JACOB is to be interpreted as our Lord. And the lambs on which there were the marks were JACOB, and those on which there were [Fol. 75*b*, col. 2] no marks were LABAN. Those on whom, as he saith, there was no mark are the Christians who have no mark of the Trinity on them. and those which have no mark are the lambs of LABAN, the 'ARAMÎ (SYRIAN), and have not in them the Faith of the Trinity.

And JOSEPH is the symbol of the Son. And that thou mayest find the day of the birth of JOSEPH, take the number of his twelve

---

[1] The Eucharistic consecration.

brethren, and the name of his father, and the name of his mother, and his own name. And then the Epact, one, and *barakat* three, and reject seven twice, and there will remain seven, which is the day of the birth of JOSEPH, on the seventh day of NAḤASSÊ. And at daybreak on that day our Lord asked His disciples and said unto them, 'What do men say of Me?' (Matt. xvi. 15; Mark x. 29; Luke ix. 20).

JOSEPH was sold for twenty [pieces of] silver [Fol. 76a, col. 1], and our Lord was sold for thirty [pieces of] silver.

As to the seven years of plenty, and the seven years of famine which JOSEPH explained, the period of famine is a symbol of the days before the coming of our Lord, and the period of plenty symbolize the days after the coming of our Lord. For before the coming of our Lord the nations lacked the meat of righteousness and the drink of righteousness. JOSEPH was the steward of EGYPT, and our Lord was the new steward of the order of things. JOSEPH dwelt in the prison-house for three years, and our Lord dwelt in the land of EGYPT for three years and seven months, from the time when He fled from [before] the face of HEROD. And again, the three years wherein He preached the word of the Gospel was a symbol of His imprisonment.

And about JOSEPH his brethren said concerning him [Fol. 76a, col. 2], 'an evil beast hath devoured him' (Gen. xxxvii. 20). Now verily these men whilst wishing to lie about his being [alive] spake against themselves, when they said 'an evil beast hath devoured him' seeing that they themselves had sold their brother. Because of this JOHN the Baptist said unto those who came to him, 'Scribes and Pharisees, a generation of beasts (*or*, vipers), who hath informed you, and who hath told you to escape from the tribulation which is to come' (Matt. iii. 7). 'Behold now, the axe is already laid to the root of the tree.' The axe of which he speaketh is the word of God, and the root of the tree of which he speaketh are the kings of the nations. This is the discourse which we have recorded concerning the work of JOSEPH, and this is the discourse on JOSEPH who was a symbol of our Lord, to whom be praise. Amen, and Amen.

[ISRAEL IN EGYPT]

And again we will also describe [to you] the dispensation which God ordained for the children of [Fol. 76b, col. 1] ISRAEL, when they were living in the land of EGYPT. And He said unto them, 'Let a man take a ram on the tenth day of the first month, and it shall be kept carefully until the fourteenth day, and he shall slay it on the fourteenth day, at the time of the turn of the evening of the thirteenth day, which shall dawn on the fourteenth day, and which shall dawn on the fifteenth. And he shall not eat thereof, and he shall not eat what is left' (Exod. xxix). Behold the explanation [of this ram].

The head of the ram is the divine voice of JESUS CHRIST. The hair (*or*, hide) of the ram is the gift of the Holy Spirit, which filleth the faithful with fervent heat. And his right fore-leg are the Twelve Apostles, and his left fore-leg the Prophets, ABRAHAM, ISAAC, and JACOB. And his right foot are the Seventy-two disciples, the Three Hundred and Eighteen orthodox Fathers, and the five hundred companions. And his left foot [Fol. 76b, col. 2] are those who [came] after them, the five hundred, in Constantinople, and the two hundred who were in EPHESUS—bishops. And his ears were the prophets, and his eyes the archbishops and bishops, the priests, and deacons, and sub-deacons, and the readers. And when a man confesseth his sins to the priest he absolveth him, and speaking putteth on the Cross, and with the mouth of the Holy Spirit, and the priest measureth his penitence, and because of him a great festival taketh place in heaven.

And the two horns of the ram are symbols of the two kingdoms of the righteous. The first of their kingdoms is the Holy Church, and the second of their kingdoms is in DABRA ṢEYÔN. And in the new world he who hath not [Fol. 77a, col. 1] come into the Church will not be able to enter DABRA ṢEYÔN and the new world [itself]. And the tail of the ram are the righteous who shall lift up testimony in the days of the False CHRIST. And behold, his intestines are the words of the Holy Scriptures, which declare the innermost things of God. And the two nostrils of the ram breathe the fervour of their faith into the holy martyrs. This ram is the symbol of JESUS CHRIST to whom be praise! Amen.

[THE TABERNACLE OF MOSES]

Concerning the fashioning of the tabernacle thus did God command MOSES: And he said unto him, 'Make for the tabernacle ten curtains, and the number of its length [shall be] one hundred [cubits], and the length of each curtain shall be twenty-eight [cubits]. Five curtains shall be supported (i.e. joined) together by the covering part in front [Fol. 77a, col. 2], and the four loops shall be looped together at their borders, and six(?) shall couple it together, and the boards thereof shall be twenty. And the hooks (or, couplings) which are in each shall be fifty. And make twelve sockets, and two boards(?): both sides(?) to one pillar. The explanation of the ten hooks is as follows:

It is as great (or, extensive) as the Church . . . the tabernacle is a symbol, and the explanation of it is the souls of the righteous. The ten couplings are symbols of the ten groups of the saints. The fifty couplings of which he speaketh are the water of the house, and the water of frankincense is the Holy Spirit which came down fifty days after the Resurrection of our Lord. And the five couplings (or, hooks) in the coverings(?) of which he speaketh are two eyes, and the hearing of two ears, and one mouth; thus the explanation of the five is completed, also the five loops which tie them all [Fol. 77*b*, col. 1].

The . . . pillars of which he speaketh are symbols of the Five [Books of] MOSES, and these are the measure of the Books. The two boards of which he speaketh as the base of a pillar are the symbols of those who are sealed with the Body and Blood of the One. The tenon of which he speaketh meaneth *'agobar*, and the sockets are the *marabâ*. The tabernacle meaneth the house of ISRAEL, and the . . . is the priest, and the couplings (*or*, hooks) thereof are those who accept the tabernacle. The forty-two pillars facing the sea are symbols of the forty-two offspring of the fathers whom MATTHEW, the Evangelist, mentioneth, and the fifteen pillars on the north side are symbols of the fifteen prophets.

The house of the altar of which he speaketh is the house of work (workshop).

The four horns of the altar of which he speaketh are symbols of the Four Evangelists [Fol. 77*b*, col. 2].

And the ash-pan of which he speaketh is the emptying-out place of the flesh. And the fire-basket, with heads(?) of iron, which is the. . . . And the grate for the west side where the fire lodgeth, and its length [of the court] shall be one hundred [cubits], and its network of brass. And the hooks and its fittings shall be of gold. And there shall be fourteen pillars in front of the face of the network and the oil of the lamp.

The vessel in which is the fire is the symbol of our Lady MARY, on whom dwelt the fire of life. And the network of brass of which he speaketh, and the horns of brass, are the symbol of the Holy Cross.

And the hooks (*or*, couplings) of gold of which he speaketh are the symbol of the priesthood.

The ten pillars of which he speaketh are the Ten Commandments.

The Vestments of the High Priest

And the oil of the lamp of which he speaketh [Fol. 78a, col. 1] is the symbol of the Faith, which hath illumined the whole world.

And the four garments of AARON, the ephod which he weareth on the Sabbath, and the *Ḳâs* which he weareth on the days of the period of the laws, and the *Ḳîdâres* (mitre) which he weareth on the days of commemoration. And the priests shall put on an *'Agê* of black silk when they purge themselves. And he shall put on a *Lagyôn* on the seven days of their festivals.

In the place of the five garments of AARON our Lord put on the garments of poverty, and humility, and mercy, and the forgiveness of sins, and commandment (*or*, authority). And the beasts which were made (*or* wrought) in the apparel of AARON, and were of pure gold, were symbols of the people who sprang from the gold of the Faith. And the girdle which was about his loins, that is *serâwêr*, [Fol. 78a, col. 2] is the symbol of the spear which speared Him. And the mitre of our [Lord] was the symbol of their mitres, and the tonsure of the heads of gold, and silver, and iron. And the tonsure of the heads of the monks are symbols of the crown of thorns which they bound on the head of our Lord.

And as to the twelve gems which were carved on in order (*or*, in a row): four stones were inscribed with the names of the children of ISRAEL, and four of the stones whereof he speaketh were symbols of the Four Gospels, and the Twelve [stones] of the children of JACOB were symbols of the Twelve Apostles.

The *Marged* of JUDAH. From the tribe of JUDAH sprang JOHN and JAMES his brother. And as the *Marged* is white, even so the flesh of JOHN the white was pure.

And the *Serdeyôn*, of a red colour, is ISSACHAR. And MATTHEW, the Evangelist, [Fol. 78b, col. 1] who described the human nature of the Son, went forth from the tribe of ISSACHAR. Now He took the form of a red man from our Lady MARY.

The Precious Stones in Aaron's Breastplate

And the *Pazyôn* (topaz?) is a symbol of the division of ZEBULON. And PHILIP went forth [from the tribe of ZEBULON] and he was the witness of His (CHRIST'S) death on the Cross. And he brought his goodness to His Creator and gave forth his fruit.

And the *'Iyâspîdes* (jasper?) had the three flaws of REUBEN in it. And from the house of REUBEN went forth 'APÎṬRÔS with ANDREW his brother. The three flaws (*or*, holes) of which he speaketh are the three denials of PETER. And they are like the coals [of fire] of SIMON, and the coals [of fire] of the jealousy of the house of SIMON, who were the Scribes and Pharisees who were jealous of the Creator, who is the Lord.

And the *Sanpêr* (sapphire) which . . . in honey(?), was GÂD [Fol. 78*b*, col. 2]. And from the tribe of GÂD went forth JACOB (JAMES) . . . who is 'ELFEYÔS (ALPHAEUS). And as the *Sanpêr* . . . in honey. So JAMES completed his martyrdom.

And the *Kêrlemâyôn* (carnelian?) is JOSEPH, and it is the stone of JOSEPH. And the interpretation of *Kêrlemâyôn* is 'making wheat to ripen in a single day'. And this word is to be interpreted by THADDEUS.

And the *'Amêsṭîs* is BENJAMIN, and it meaneth 'Apostle of the nations (Gentiles)'; and this word is to be interpreted by PAUL.

And the *'Akṭîs* is EPHRAIM, and it is the same as *'Akwâs* and the same as *Mam'ĕl*. And this word is to be interpreted by MATTHEW.

And the *Sûbâwê* is NAPHTALI. *Sûbâwê* means 'vine cluster'. And this word is to be interpreted by BARTHOLOMEW.

And the *Karesîlôtô* (chrysolite?) [Fol. 79*a*, col. 1], that is the 'stone of gold' is the stone of DÂN. And from his tribe went forth JUDAS ISCARIOT. He speaketh of gold because [our Lord] appointed JUDAS to be the custodian of the bag of money. And the Evangelist calleth him ISCARIOT because of this, for he had charge of the bag, and was the steward of the gifts and charities.

And *Bîrôlê* meaneth 'lamp', and this is the stone of ASHER, and the two words may be interpreted by THOMAS, who is the lamp spoken of. For like a lamp he illumined the doctrine of the twins, and THOMAS meaneth the sun.

Such is the interpretation (*or*, explanation) of the gems which were in the apparel of AARON the priest.

And the garments which AARON wore over his shoulders and breast are to be interpreted by the cords which they threw about the neck of our Lord [Fol. 79*a*, col. 2]. The former describeth the latter, and the latter fulfilleth the former. Praise be unto the Creator of the Universe! Amen.

And as concerneth the position of AARON about which he speaketh, even thus was it. The explanation of the one which was burnt outside: It was the symbol of CHRIST who was killed outside the camp. And the four horns of the altar that were sprinkled with blood, of which he speaketh, are the four archbishops who were sprinkled with the blood of CHRIST. And the girdle of his belly is to be interpreted by the assembly of the Apostles. And the two kidneys of which he speaketh are to be interpreted by PETER and PAUL. And the two rams of which he speaketh are to be explained by CHRIST. And the blood which filled the sanctuary is to be explained by the blood of CHRIST which hath filled the Church. And the cutting off of the limbs and members of the ram of which he speaketh [Fol. 79*b*, col. 1] symbolize the mutilation of our Lord, and of the Apostles in their companies, and the martyrs in their companies, and the monks in their companies, and the priests in their companies. And as to the washing of the viscera [of the ram] with water, of which he speaketh, the viscera are the offspring of the liver(?), and thou shalt place them as close as possible to his head; thus meaneth the body of our Lord which is in the patera in the hand. And in that he saith, 'thou shalt lift up the whole body of the ram on to the

The Giving of Alms

altar', he meaneth that our Lord JESUS CHRIST was offered as a gift to His Father, and that He offereth up incense and glorious sacrifices to His Father. And the ram which was complete is the symbol of the Lord. And the blood which was poured on the tip of his (AARON'S) ear is the symbol of the blood of CHRIST [Fol. 79b, col. 2] wherewith the faithful shall be anointed. And as the first thing of all the anointing of the hand maketh complete the office of the priests of the Gospel. And the breast of the ram of which he speaketh is the *samsam* whereon spring out the teats of the breast. And the two rams [which are to be offered] continually, that of the morning and that of the evening, are to be interpreted by the prayers of the saints which the angels offer up evening and morning. And immediately the cocks crow the angels burst into song. And the five fine linen *sarâyek* may be explained as the five wise virgins.

And the garment of network made of gold brocade is the symbol of *'altâḥ*, and it is a garment of four colours; it is the symbol of the four figures which were inlaid on the apparel of our Lord. And the broad band of netting round the garment *lôgyôdâ*(?) which [AARON] weareth is what the SERÂPHÎM array themselves in on great days [of festivals].

[Fol. 80a, col. 1.] And the red flower of the pomegranate is the symbol of the shedding of the blood of the martyrs. And this [is the end of] the symbolism of MOSES.

And concerning the [giving of] alms God commanded MOSES that a man should bring [them], and he said unto him:

'Let every man bring alms'; and they brought them. The Twelve Angels of night are the symbols of the Twelve Angels who are the Apostles. And that which they brought to each of the angels was a *kual*. Alms—one *berûr* (silver) equals one hundred and thirty *ḥasbû*. One *feyal* of silver equals seventy-one shekels, according to the shekel of the sanctuary. The *maḍab*, which is the *gayba* of gold. The twelve

157

gold [pieces] which he speaketh of are one *sêtu*. And he speaketh of the *khasabû* because it is made to go forth for one hundred and thirty men, and the seventy shekels because it is made to go forth for seventy men. And the alms of which he speaketh of again [Fol. 80*a*, col. 2] is the symbol of his father ADAM of whom God said, 'My similitude and my likeness'. The *feyâl* (silver coins) are *kenberât*. And concerning this SOLOMON saith, 'If of *feyâl* coins thou hast given to him, at a later period in thine own eyes, thy nakedness shall travel(?) like brass.'

And now, let us come back to the beginning of the matter of the bowl (laver) [made of] twenty (*sic*) . . . of gold. The bowl is the symbol of CHRIST, the laver of life. The ten . . . of gold of which he speaketh are the ten fingers of the hands of our Lord which were spread out on the wood of the Cross.

The incense inside it of which he speaketh is the prayer of the saints. And as ABÛ ḲALAMSÎS saith, 'He gave him censers(?) that he might transmit the prayers of all [Fol. 80*b*, col. 1] the saints.

The fat ox of which he speaketh is CHRIST Himself.

The ram of which he speaketh is the ram CHRIST, and that [thou mayest know] that the ram is CHRIST, hear what ISAIAH saith, 'He came, that He might be slaughtered like a lamb.'

The fleshy ram of which he speaketh is the symbol of CHRIST who was burdened with human flesh.

The five . . . of which he speaketh are the five . . . of the slave(?)

The five goats are the five princes of PHILISTIA, GATH, ASKELON, GÂZÂ, EKRÔN.

And the five ewes of which he speaketh are the symbols of the five wise virgins.

And the two cocks of which he speaketh are the symbols of the peoples of EDOM and the tribes of MOAB who were called unto the Faith. Concerning MOAB the Holy Spirit saith, 'MOAB is the priest

The Tâbôt (*Ark of the Covenant*) *was Mary the Virgin*

[Fol. 80*b*, col. 2] of my hope.' And concerning EDOM he saith, 'Over EDOM I will cast my shoe' (Ps. lx. 8). The shoe he speaketh of concerneth the holy Christians, who shall be spread out among the nations, and the priest who is present is the Son of God who is over all nations.

The opening (*madkeh*) of the tabernacle is the symbol of Him that is to come. And instead of those who shall come the opening in the first Law which He hath shown us is the reward of the Church. And instead of the opening of the tabernacle of which He speaketh is the singing of the Saints. The opening of which He speaketh meaneth *sawâlek*, and this is the covering of the TÂBÔT. And the word ram which he useth here, and in sundry other places, is equivalent to saying 'symbol of the Trinity'.

And the gold censer is the symbol of the Only One. And the incense and the smoke of the [Fol. 81*a*, col. 1] vapour which it sendeth up from it indicateth the sufferings of CHRIST who offered up to His Father incense and glorious (*or,* precious) offerings. And concerning this SOLOMON saith—with reference to the soul of CHRIST, 'What is this which goeth up from the desert like a germ of the smoke of incense?' He saith unto thee, 'From the desert' so that what He Himself said should come to pass. Behold He went up to JERUSALEM and they crucified the Son of man. And as in this place the smoke which went forth from the burning, even so many sufferings went forth from the Lord. He was seized. He was hung on the Cross. He suffered fever. He was buffeted and beaten. His back was scourged, and instead of water He drank vinegar, and the decree of death came to Him. And in His sufferings He censed the throne of His Father.

The TÂBÔT [Fol. 81*a*, col. 2] in which was the . . . is the symbol of our Lady MARY. And the Ten Commandments which were in the TÂBÔT were the symbol of CHRIST, the splendour of life; the Word

159

of the Father. Verily, He was a man and He chose our Lady MARY, virgin in her body and virgin in her mind, and virgin in her mouth, and virgin in her eyes. In her body there was no blemish. And in her mind she thought no evil thing, for the Holy Spirit was her guardian and her protector. Her mouth never spoke evil, and her eyes were never closed with evil intent. These four kinds of virginity do we find with our Lady MARY. Whereas with men, there is none perfect, for all men are corrupt either in their bodies or their minds. And the mind [Fol. 81b, col. 1] of the angel is not equal in purity with that of the mind of our Lady MARY.

This is the whole of the discourse on the Tabernacle.

[MOSES AND HIS SUCCESSORS]

We will make clear the matter of MOSES. He was born on the thirteenth day of NAHASSÊ. He hath no Epact number. And he was the symbol of the Son. And JOB, father of the patient endurance of the Son, was the symbol of the Son. And 'ÎYÂSÛ (JOSHUA) . . . was the symbol of the Son. And he was born when there was no Epact on the . . . of the month of TÂKHSHÂSH. Now observe that his appearance was very plainly that of the Son.

As when JOSHUA came ISRAEL inherited the land of promise, even so Christians have inherited the Holy Church. So JOSHUA had the style and eyes of two men, and they were symbols of the 'ÔRÎT and the Prophets.

And RÂBE'A was the symbol of the Church. The red cord [Fol. 81b, col. 2] which she tied to the window of her house, was the symbol of the blood which poured from the side of our Lord. And CANAAN was delivered over unto the hand of JOSHUA [as] the devils were delivered over into the hand of the Lord. And as in the days of JOSHUA the sun stood still for one day, [which] became two, as on the day of the crucifixion of our Lord, one day became two. JOSHUA took the sign of a perfect sun. JOSHUA chose twelve stones, and JESUS chose Twelve Apostles. JOSHUA chose seven festival horns to sound, and the Lord JESUS seven chiefs of the Church. With JOSHUA in his days there was found 'AKÂR (ACHAN) the thief, and with the Lord in His days was found JUDAS the thief of the money bag. To JOSHUA in his days [Fol. 82a, col. 1] the hearts of all the children of ISRAEL were in subjection, and to our Lord JESUS CHRIST Christian people were in subjection with one heart and one Faith. In the days of JOSHUA the people forsook the worship of MAGÔRGÂR, and in the days of JESUS the people forsook the worship of idols. JOSHUA divided the land and gave to every tribe its proper territory, and CHRIST ruled the Church, and ruled the Christians, assigning to them their grades and their positions. In the days of JOSHUA what was good took place, and in the days of JESUS His people inherited the Kingdom of the heavens. In the days of JOSHUA the things which were wished for in battle took place, and in the days of JESUS the [Fol. 82a, col. 2] holy Apostles were made ready to become martyrs. And this is what JOSHUA, the son of NUN, desired(?) for us, and it became the shadow and the similitude of the new Law.

[DAVID THE ANCESTOR OF CHRIST]

Here is the discourse concerning DAVID, the son of JESSE. In order to find the birth[day] of DAVID, take the number ten, and the name of his father and the name of his mother, and the number fifty, and reject (divide?) by sevens the whole number. And what remaineth is the birth[day] of DAVID on the seventh day of MÎYÂZYÂR. DAVID was born on the same day as ADAM. And he was the symbol of the Son, and according to the flesh, he was called the father of our Lord, because our Lady MARY was descended from DAVID. And he prophesied that He would come, and that He would be born, and that He would be crucified and would rise [again]. And concerning the

Trinity [Fol. 82*b*, col. 1] he prophesied deep things and said, 'Who is the Lord except God? And who is God except the Lord, who hath girded me with strength?' Observe now that God hath spoken unto thee twice concerning the Trinity. And he also saith concerning the Trinity, 'I have sought Thy face; Thy face Lord will I seek'. 'And turn not Thy face from me.' And again he saith, 'My Lord sayeth to the Lord, Sit thou on my right hand' with reference to the Trinity. And again he saith, 'I will go in to the altar of God, to my God, so that I may rejoice my youth. I will praise Thee, O my God, on the harp,' and this also indicateth the Trinity. And again he saith concerning this, 'I will(?) anoint . . . Lord . . . my God [Fol. 82*b*, col. 2] out of gladness . . . of those who are like unto thee.' And 'those who are like unto thee', of whom he speaketh are the prophets. And he saith, 'my God' because He put on the flesh of man. Observe how the Trinity is indicated in this passage. And He himself saith 'Lord', indicating His Trinity. I will go up into heaven to My Father, and my 'Father' is as your God. Thus doth DAVID say concerning the Trinity, To Him be praise, the Maker of all creation, for ever and ever.

Amen and Amen.

APPENDIX

A LIST OF THE PASSAGES
FROM THE OLD AND NEW TESTAMENTS QUOTED OR
REFERRED TO IN THE WORKS OF BAKHAYLA MÎKÂ'ÊL

Y

List of Passages

Index

Index

Earth, the creation of the, 13; the division of the, 91-2.

'Êdôm, the Garden of, created, 15.

Edomites, the, 109, 158, 159.

Effigies of the saints, the, 70; of the patriarchs, 71.

'Egâlêmûn, an angel, 28.

Egypt, 88; Israel in, 151-2.

Egyptians, the, 34-5, 109.

'Egzi'beḥêr, God, 6, 8.

Ekrôn, the prince of, 158.

'êksedrê, baskets, 53.

'êlâm, vestibule, pillar, 53, 55.

'Êl'âzâr, 111.

'Êldâ, 148.

Eldridge, E., ix.

Elephant, Adam mounted on an, 21-2.

'Êlfâsâfî, 67.

'Elfeyôs, Alphaeus, 155.

'Êlî, 120.

Elias, 38.

Elijah, 70, 89, 95, 111, 121.

Elisabeth, 113.

'Êlyas, Elijah, 111.

'Êlyâs, olive, 139.

'Êlyazâr, 65.

'Elyô, an angel, 28.

Emerald, the, as a symbol, 72, 73.

'Enbâḳôm, Habakkuk, 112.

'Enbarâm, 65, 110.

'Êngûtât tree, the, 139.

Enoch, 18, 34, 36, 39, 61, 89, 108, 109; the book of, v, vi, xiv-xviii, 141; Discourse concerning the Birth of, xx, 140-62.

'entalâm, a measure, 27, 56.

'êpêmêdê, platform, 53, 54.

Ephesians, the church of the, 100.

'Êphêsôn, the river, 132.

Ephesus, 133, 151; the archbishop of, 115.

Ephraim, 112; symbolized, 155.

'Êrmeyâs, Jeremiah, 111.

Esau, 71, 88, 89, 108, 113, 122, 149.

'Êsêdêrês, chief priest, 73.

'Êsey, Jesse, 111.

'Êsôn, 78.

Ethiopia, the kings of, 66, 90, 123.

Euphrates, the river, 116, 121, 133.

'Êrâr, the [second] heaven, 9.

Eutychians, the, 115.

Eve, 25-6, 39, 138.

'Êwâs, 110.

Ezekiel, 8, 36, 64, 66, 83, 111, 113-14, 121, 136; his vision of the Tabernacle, 51 ff.

Ezra, 54, 88, 103, 107, 111; the books of, 74; the eagle seen by, 88-9.

Fabri, Claude. See Peiresc, C. F. de.

Face, the angels of the, 11, 71.

Fâḳûrâ, 66.

False Christ, the, 123.

Fârêg, 66.

Fârêg Tâmmûz, 66.

Fâres, the country of, 133.

ferem tree, the, 9.

Festivals of Israel, the, 76-7.

feṭerat, cherubim, 44.

feyal, a coin, 157, 158.

Fire, creation out of, 9-10.

Firmament, the creation of the, 14.

Fish, the creation of, 18-19.

Flood, the, 29.

Fog, creation out of, 9.

Gabriel, the archangel, 24, 82, 99; his speech, 5 ff.; circumcised Abraham, 33; the tribe of, 86.

Gabriel Theologus, 101.

Gâd, 113; symbolized, 72

gadab (galab), fish-hook, 27.

Gâdî, king, 89.

Gahânam, Gehenna, 23, 54, 55.

Gâlân, 79; the daughter of, 78.

Gâlê, an angel, 27.

Games, the origin of, 28.

Gânên, devil, 116.

Gargê, an angel, 27.

Gassendi, Peter, his life of Peiresc, v, xiii-xiv.

Gath, the prince of, 158.

Gawaz tree, the, 139.

gayba, a measure, 157.

Gâydâd, 142.

Gâzâ, the prince, 158.

Geba'êl, 112.

Gebeṣ, Egyptian, 31.

Gëëz language, the, 147.

George the Syncellus, xvi, xviii.

Gêrgêl, the [first] heaven, 8.

Gêrsam, 65.

Geyôn, the river, 133-4.

Giants, the destruction of the, 29.

Gibeon, 119.

Gilles de Loches, xiv.

Gîmêr, an angel, 28.

Godhead, Discourse concerning the Mystery of the, xx, 6, 126-7; the attributes of the, 14.

Gold, the symbolism of, 43.

Gôtôlyâl (?), 113.

Governors (angels), the creation of the, 12.

Gray, L. H., 98 n.

Guidi, Prof. D. Ignazio, his work on the MS., vii, xx.

169

Index

Index

Index

172

Index

Index

174

Index

175